CRYPTOMARKETS

EMERALD STUDIES IN DIGITAL CRIME, TECHNOLOGY AND SOCIAL HARMS

Series Editors

James Martin, Swinburne University of Technology, Australia

Asher Flynn, School of Social Sciences, Monash University, Australia

Over the past two decades, digital technologies have come to permeate ever more aspects of contemporary life. This trend looks set to continue and has profound implications for the social sciences, particularly criminology, with technology-facilitated offences now arguably constituting the most dynamic and rapidly growing area of contemporary crime. Despite this development, the discipline of criminology has been slow to embrace the critical study of technology-facilitated offences and social harms, with most research conducted in this area still informed by a relatively narrow range of cybersecurity and applied criminological perspectives.

Emerald Studies in Digital Crime, Technology and Social Harms is part of a new movement within criminology and related disciplines to broaden this narrow focus and engage critically with new trends in technology-facilitated offending and victimisation. The book series uses a combination of critical criminological, socio-legal and sociological perspectives to consider a wide range of technology-facilitated offences and harmful social practices, ranging from digital surveillance, cyber-bullying and image-based sexual abuse through to global darknet drug trading.

EDITORIAL BOARD

CRYPTOMARKETS: A RESEARCH COMPANION

BY

JAMES MARTIN
JACK CUNLIFFE
RASMUS MUNKSGAARD

emerald PUBLISHING

United Kingdom – North America – Japan – India
Malaysia – China

Emerald Publishing Limited
Howard House, Wagon Lane, Bingley BD16 1WA, UK

First edition 2019

British Library Cataloguing in Publication Data
A catalogue record for this book is available from the British Library

ISBN: 978-1-83867-033-7 (Print)
ISBN: 978-1-83867-030-6 (Online)
ISBN: 978-1-83867-032-0 (Epub)

To the cryptomarket community.

CONTENTS

LIST OF FIGURES AND TABLES

Figures

Table

ACKNOWLEDGEMENTS

This book was written with the generous contribution of a host of people whose insights, support and feedback are most gratefully appreciated. In particular, we would like to acknowledge and thank Jules Wilan and the rest of the publishing team at Emerald, Judith Aldridge, David Décary-Hétu, Nicholas Christin, Caleb and Gwern Branwen. Penultimately, we wish to thank the friends, families and loved ones of each of us for their support, patience and all of the other day-to-day acts of kindness upon which every author ultimately depends. Lastly, we wish to thank each of those members of the academy comprising the cryptomarket research community. This book is a reflection of your work more than ours and would not have been possible without you.

INTRODUCTION

This book is about cryptomarkets and cryptomarket research, with a particular focus on the illicit drugs trade. As the title suggests, it is intended as a guidebook to those with an interest in conducting their own study into this fascinating and ever-expanding area of research. There is no shortage of interesting fodder. In little more than eight years, cryptomarkets have facilitated hundreds of thousands illicit drug exchanges, likely worth in excess of two billion US dollars. They have been implicated in fatal overdoses and facilitate door-to-door delivery of a greater volume and wider range of illicit drugs than may be witnessed in any open air drug market in the world, and yet they are widely suspected to be reducing a range of systemic drug and prohibition-related harms. They have been linked to acts of domestic terrorism (Malik, 2019), been falsely implicated in providing a safe haven for hitmen (Ormsby, 2016) and traders in weapons of mass destruction (Brewster, 2017) and caused both media sensations and moral panics on both sides of the Atlantic, and as far afield as Australia and Argentina. They have catalysed the development of new investigative tools and strategies, and new forms of transnational policing, jurisprudence and cross-jurisdictional extradition. And each year they grow bigger, demonstrating a remarkable resilience to internal and external assaults reminiscent of the mythical hydra of antiquity.

As we said, no shortage of fodder.

Overarching all of this has been the development of an entirely new sub-field of research – cryptomarket studies – which has seen extraordinary methodological development and innovation across a diverse range of disciplines, including criminology, sociology, computer science, economics and public health. There is room for more. Indeed, more studies, more grants, more researchers – whether undergraduate, post-graduate, doctoral or professorial – and the involvement of more disciplines and cross-disciplinary collaborations. These are sorely needed to extend the field further and to help understand what are truly twenty-first century phenomena: anonymous online marketplaces with operations and implications that stretch around the globe and into the deepest recesses of cyberspace.

So, to accompany this scholarly call to arms (or, more accurately, keyboards), we present this book, which comprises four distinct chapters, each intended to assist cryptomarket research in some way. Chapter 1 provides a history of the development of cryptomarkets. It grounds our understanding of these unique online phenomena within an economic-sociological framework and discusses how cryptomarkets emerged as a social institution with their own norms, processes and political ideologies. The chapter separates cryptomarket history into three broad epochs, with a preceding section focused on the period prior to the launch of Silk Road and concluding with the seemingly permanent state of flux following the massive transnational policing crackdown, Operation Onymous.

Chapter 2 provides a detailed overview of the current state of cryptomarket research with a focus on macro-level empirical trends and developments. These include estimates of the overall size and composition of the cryptomarket economy;

its geographical distribution and effects on drug trafficking routes and organised crime groups; and the various stages comprising the cryptomarket lifecycle, as well as the leading causes of their mortality. Also included in this chapter is a qualitative analysis of non-drug goods and services and market prohibitions. Here, free from the governing influence of any state or (legal) corporate power, the communities surrounding cryptomarkets – from market administrators to anonymous purchasers of drugs, guns or credit cards – reveal their values, ethics and limits of toleration.

In Chapter 3, we provide a detailed analysis of the various methodologies by which cryptomarkets are understood by the academic community. These include quantitative approaches, such as surveys and the use of automated software crawlers which collect and parse the digital traces left lingering on the dark web by tens, perhaps hundreds, of thousands of pseudonymous traders. Discussed also are qualitative approaches, from lurking on markets and discussion forums, to deep ethnography and interview techniques requiring the active participation and consent of one of the most elusive subject populations in the digital world. The use of both new and old research methods necessitates ethical consideration and reflection, which are also detailed and debated in the final section of the chapter, with particular reference to the often-conflicting needs of the academy and law enforcement.

Chapter 4, the conclusion of the book, discusses the limits of our knowledge and understanding of cryptomarkets. It outlines trends and activities which we suspect to be occurring, but have not yet confirmed or disproved, highlights research areas that are neglected or underdeveloped and offers a suite of questions, topics and hypotheses for future research.

As will become clear throughout the book, much has been achieved in recent years in our understanding cryptomarkets, but there is still much more to do. Presented herein are all of the tools, techniques and backgrounds information we believe are necessary to begin one's foray into the cryptomarket research space. We hope that you find it a useful starting point for the exciting journey ahead.

1

A MODERN-DAY HISTORY OF CRYPTOMARKETS

1.1. OVERVIEW

This chapter aims to detail the historical trajectory of the cryptomarket. To do so necessitates some reflection on the correct choice of words and the framing that is implicit to sketching out such a history. Should we consider the cryptomarket a radical re-organisation of the online drug trade? Should we see it as the fulfilment of crypto-anarchist prophecies of the inevitability of black markets online? Or should we merely consider it another iteration of a social practice, the trade of illicit goods online, which dates back to the first days of the internet. This is a matter of perspective, and this chapter remains cautious, leaving it to the reader to draw their own conclusions. This cautious approach sees the cryptomarket, paraphrasing its original designer and implementer, *as the putting together of pieces* that already existed. Thus, we propose that this was neither an inevitable outcome nor that the cryptomarket emerged from a social and political vacuum.

We separate the historical trajectory of cryptomarkets into three distinct phases, or *epochs*, and a prelude, for analytical purposes. As the proceeding chapters will show, trends and structural change cannot be isolated into distinct phases, but they do provide a frame of reference. We begin by sketching out the historical, social and political context from which the cryptomarket emerged, and proceed to introduce and discuss the history of illicit markets online, showing that these were flourishing even before the cryptomarket. We then consider the first epoch as the rise of Silk Road and the emergence of the cryptomarket, with the second phase marked by the chaos ensuing the fall of Silk Road. Finally, we discuss the current epoch – which we argue in Chapter 4 is still current. Briefly, these may be considered epochs marked by *emergence*, *reconfiguration* and *settlement*. Each of these were distinguished by different academic approaches, which are detailed more in proceeding chapters, and particular sets of challenges posed to cryptomarket denizens, whether they are buyers, admins or vendors. We limit ourselves from discussing first the 'drama' and intrigues of backstage cryptomarket activity, and the minute details of police investigations – to do so would simply be too long winded. The intricacies of the police investigations into Silk Road, the alleged murders-for-hire, and the conspiratorial sentiments surrounding the Silk Road trial are beyond the scope of this book, and the interested reader is directed to Ormsby (2014) for more detail. Rather, we focus on the broad changes and movements of cryptomarket history.

Some scholars have suggested cryptomarkets represent a new generation of illicit markets, an evolutionary stage (Przepiorka, Norbutas, & Corten, 2017), while others see them as proposing solutions for the problems that haunt illicit markets (Bakken, Moeller, & Sandberg, 2018; Moeller, Munksgaard, & Demant, 2017; Tzanetakis, 2018a). We propose neither a reconciliation nor a synthesis of these propositions but suggest a conceptualisation of the cryptomarket as a social institution drawing upon the new economic sociology (Granovetter, 1992, 2017), a conceptualisation that is compatible with both perspectives. Reflecting on the history of the cryptomarket, we argue that in the years following the implementation of Silk Road, we have seen a process of institutionalisation, in which a stable set of norms, behaviours and attitudes have settled *a way of doing business*. While the story of the cryptomarket continues, the mood amongst scholars and amongst some in the cryptomarket community itself seems to have settled on the rather mundane conclusion that not much seems to have changed since Silk Road. Markets still resemble Silk Road and despite the perceived threats to the system of the reconfiguration that distinguished the second epoch the technology very much remains the same. Most scholars no longer expect widespread adoption of technological advances like decentralised markets, nor do we expect mass adoption of sophisticated solutions to problems inherent in the centralised escrow model of cryptomarkets. Rather, the changes we expect to see in the cryptomarket, as we discuss in the final chapter, are an increasing overlap with the offline drug economy, and apart from that, *business as usual* with perhaps some slight change around the edges to account for unexpected shocks.

1.2. THE 'CALM', OR *ANARCHY*, BEFORE THE STORM

The original cryptomarket, *Silk Road*, did not emerge in a vacuum inventing an online drug trade where none had existed before and nor did it invent the technologies upon which it is dependent. Rather, in the words of its administrator, Dread Pirate Roberts, 'everything was in place, he just put the pieces together'[1] (Greenberg, 2013). As such, a history of the cryptomarket necessitates an understanding of the history that came before the first post on the Bitcoin Talk forum that announced Silk Road to the wider world (Buxton & Bingham, 2015). Broadly, we may separate these antecedents of the cryptomarket under two broad themes: The online drug trade and the social, political, technological and organisational roots of *Silk Road.*

Before *Silk Road* and dating back to what preceded the internet, ARPANET, the sale of unregulated or illegal goods sale been a staple of the internet dating back to the 1960s (Walsh, 2011) and the first item ever to have been traded online was cannabis between graduate students (Markoff, 2005). As the internet has become ubiquitous, so has illicit online markets – which have emerged, vanished, and remained in a variety of forms: The sale of drugs on public social media (Moyle, Childs, Coomber, & Barratt, 2019; Stevens, 2016), the trade in stolen goods (Aniello & Caneppele, 2018), the sale of products associated with the wildlife trade (Lavorgna, 2014), and a range of illegal markets catering to the growing industry around credit card fraud and hacking are but some examples (e.g. Hutchings & Holt, 2017; Soudijn & Zegers, 2012).

The sale of illicit drugs online grew particularly in the years after 2000 as *new psychoactive substances* (NPS) were increasingly sold online (Orsolini, Francesconi, Papanti, Giorgetti, & Schifano et al., 2015). Often in a legal grey area, being neither illegal nor controlled but with psychoactive effects, the internet provided an easy way of distributing substances like Mephedrone, synthetic cannabinoids or psychedelics like 2C-B (EMCDDA & Europol, 2016; Martinez, Kmetonyová, & Běláčková, 2016). Likewise, performance enhancers (both mental and physical), steroids and prescription medicine also became readily available online during this period (Krebs, 2014; Littlejohn, Baldacchino, Schifano, & Deluca, 2005; Orsolini et al., 2015). Generally, these markets for drugs utilised single actor web shops on the regular internet (clear web) and allowed for electronic payments, mimicking licit online stores. As such, the online trade in psychoactive substances and drugs was not a novel phenomenon when *Silk Road* launched (as will be discussed in Section 1.3.1).

As the internet and online commerce grew to become ubiquitous a movement of hackers, activists and cryptographers, parts of a growing 'digiterati' (Ludlow, 2001), discussed, wrote and implemented technologies that sought to mitigate what was seen as almost inevitable exploitation of the internet for surveillance purposes and governmental regulation (May, 2001a, 2001b). While no one coherent political ideology can be identified for this movement or ethos, its ideological foundations can be traced back to a peculiar combination of politics 'reconciling the anarchism of the New Left with the entrepreneurial zeal of the New Right' (Barbrook & Cameron, 2001) – a mix of free market capitalism, opposition to governmental regulation and an adoration for values of privacy and personal choice. Noteworthy documents from this era are the *Cipherpunk FAQ*, an FAQ written by Timothy May which sought to synthesise the politics and analyses of a fragmented mailing list (May, 1994). Amongst other things, May argued for the inevitability of assassination markets (i.e. crowdfunded assassinations) and a state of anarcho-capitalism he termed *crypto-anarchy* (May, 2001b). Less radically, Perry Barlow (2001), the lyricist of The Grateful Dead, penned 'A Declaration of the Independence of Cyberspace' declaring the Internet *naturally independent of the tyrannies you [governments] seek to impose on us*. In this discursive environment, a mix of programmers, hackers, activists and cryptographers, some identifying as *cipherpunks* and crypto-anarchists, took upon themselves to begin building the technologies that would ensure the independence of cyberspace from governmental intrusion. The first *mixnets* and *remailers*, systems which allowed internet traffic and emails to be routed through a network of computers and anonymised, were developed in this context (Chaum, 1981; May, 2001a). Similarly, Phillip Zimmermann, in vehement opposition to impending mass surveillance, wrote and publicly released the PGP, *Pretty Good Privacy*, protocol for encrypting and authenticating messages, files and documents (Zimmermann, 1999). At this point, the first experiments with digital and untraceable currencies were taking place as well (Chaum, Fiat, & Naor, 1988). These technologies continued to be developed over the coming years.

Thus, when in 2011 the user *altoid* posted a link to 'The Silk Road Marketplace' on the Bitcoin Talk forums (Buxton & Bingham, 2015, p. 8), both a market for drugs and the technological building blocks of Silk Road existed. The URL to *Silk Road* ended in *.onion*, designating its status as a website that could only be accessed using the Tor network, a modern iteration of *mixnets*, effectively making the connection to a historical and political legacy explicit. Neither was it a coincidence that the link was posted on a forum dedicated to the emerging cryptocurrency Bitcoin, a decentralised, deflationary, digital and pseudonymous form of virtual cash: An implementation of May's prophecies of currencies outside state control and thus in direct extension of the *cipherpunks'* early experiments and concepts of digital cash (Golumbia, 2017; Nakamoto, 2008). *Silk Road*, of course, only accepted payment in this nascent virtual currency and was only accessible using Tor, meaning one had to 'hook in' to this technological and political legacy in order to buy illicit drugs.

1.3. SILK ROAD MARKETPLACE – A PARADIGM CHANGE

From January 2011 to October 2013, *Silk Road* reigned supreme, though not alone, on the Tor network as the principal platform offering illicit drugs (Soska & Christin, 2015; Van Buskirk, Roxburgh, Farrell, & Burns, 2014). An early competitor of Silk Road was the platform *Farmers' Market*, which had been operational since 2010 and was shut down by the FBI in 2012 (Zetter, 2012). Later on, in 2013, Atlantis Marketplace launched, mimicking the style and organisation of Silk Road, though the website announced itself using a snazzy YouTube video rather than a link on a cryptocurrency forum (Ormsby, 2014). The organisational form which Silk Road developed during its reign, both in appearance and structure (i.e. administrators, moderators, vendors and buyers), is best described as a paradigm change because it became to be widely adopted. Of course, as acknowledged by the administrator of Silk Road himself, *Dread Pirate Roberts*, *the pieces were already there*. The pieces that Dread Pirate Roberts put together in 2011 remain largely the same as today, with the basic formula of the cryptomarket changing little since that time. Grouping these pieces, we may summarise them as the *platform economy design*, *technologies for anonymisation and encryption* and *escrow and dispute resolution*.

1.3.1. An Illegal Platform Economy

The formula which *Silk Road* presented was organisationally similar to eBay, Uber, Amazon, Etsy and other *platform economies* which sell legal goods online: The website offers a platform which buyers and sellers can use in exchange for a commission and in return, administrators provide some form of governance and organisation (Christin, 2013; Langley & Leyshon, 2017; Martin, 2014a). In terms of its design *Silk Road* and later cryptomarkets were, and remain, strikingly similar to licit platform economies, specifically those which Langley and Leyshon (2017) term *online exchange markets*.

Typical functionality includes search bars, categorisation of products, and a feedback system, also known as *reputation system* (Resnick, Kuwabara, Zeckhauser, & Friedman, 2000). In comparison to previous modes of organising illicit trade online, the mimicry of licit platforms was highly innovative. Excluding trading inside closed social networks (e.g. via email or chat rooms), illicit online markets had typically taken the form of either *forums* or *shops*. The already existing Farmers' Market followed a 'forum structure' similarly to the forums used by hackers, carders and fraudsters (Lusthaus, 2012; Soudijn & Zegers, 2012; Zetter, 2012). Depending on exclusivity, such forums will typically be limited to invited guests, require some form of vetting or be completely open for registration (Dupont, Côté, Boutin, & Fernandez, 2017; Holt & Dupont, 2019). Those who are members can post and comment in threads and subforums offering, for example, goods for sale or the provision of feedback. The *shop*-format would be one seller selling their goods on a dedicated website, as was prevalent with NPS, or utilised in the fraud and carding economy in the form of *autoshops* wherein buyers can easily sort and buy stolen credit cards and associated information. It can be argued that the platform organisation of Silk Road combined these by giving individual sellers a 'storefront' while simultaneously providing the services that administrators would offer in the forums like dispute resolution and rule enforcement, combining the *shop* and *forum* formats. However, more importantly, Silk Road allowed sellers to compete side-by-side, appearing alongside each other in search results, and remained open to all.[2]

1.3.2. Encryption and Anonymity

In addition to proposing a new mode of organising illicit online markets, *Silk Road* further combined the technologies discussed in Section 1.2 and utilised in other illicit markets. Specifically, Silk Road required the use of Tor and Bitcoin, and strongly encouraged the use of PGP encryption.

First, *Silk Road* was only available using the Tor network. The experiments with anonymous internet traffic in the form of *mixnets* and *remailers* had grown in sophistication since the 1980s and 1990s, and with funding from the US Defense Advanced Research Projects Agency (DARPA) research labs, the Tor Project had developed the code and implementation for a global network of computers collaboratively giving users of the network anonymity by routing their traffic through each other (Dingledine, Syverson, Mathewson, & Syverson, 2004; Tor Project, 2019). Though Tor's primary function is the anonymisation of the origin and destination of internet traffic for the purposes of censorship avoidance and privacy, the protocol also allows the creation of *'hidden services'* or *'onion services'*, websites which can only be accessed through the network thus anonymising any visitor from surveillance by the operator of the site and any surveilling entity (Moore & Rid, 2016). Similarly, the location and IP address of the website remain hidden thereby mitigating the tools of internet regulation traditionally available to law enforcement (Goldsmith, 2000; Hutchings & Holt, 2017; Spitters, Verbruggen, & Van Staalduinen, 2014). Web services which are only accessible using specialised software (e.g. the Tor Browser) are commonly referred to as the *darknet* or *dark web*. These terms are an extension of a division originally proposed by Bergman (2001), who argued that the web can be divided into a *clear* and *deep* web, of which the former is what is available through search engines while the latter is not. In contemporary research, a coherent definition of the three is provided by Gehl (2018). Gehl suggests first and foremost the use of *web* rather than *net*, to clearly designate that the content discussed is *web*pages (i.e. markup, HTML), and then distinguishes the three as (a) content that is available through search engines, (b) content that is not available through search engines, and (c) content that requires specialised software to access.

The 'dark web' has in recent years become of great interest both in popular and academic discourse. It is, in this context, important to stress two main findings in the literature on the dark web. First, dark webs, of which hidden services on Tor constitute the largest, are but a fraction of the content available online. Estimates are difficult to establish given the short life of most websites, but Spitters et al. (2014) find 5,725 websites, Moore and Rid (2016) find 5,205, and Sanchez-Rola, Balzarotti, and Santos (2017) find 7,257. As such, it is relatively small. Further, the content on these sites span a wide continuum in terms of legality and popular legitimacy. In the entrepreneurial sector, research suggests that the largest dark web industries are the market for hacking, fraud and stolen data, and cryptomarkets (Spitters et al., 2014). These two have increasingly begun to overlap both in terms of user base and organisation (discussed in Section 1.4.2), but as such remain isolated from other illegal content. Other types of illegal or 'deviant' content found on the Tor network, and other dark webs, are child sexual exploitation material, types of pornography, writings on topics like suicide and political extremism (Moore & Rid, 2016; Mörch et al., 2018; Spitters et al., 2014). There has also been a number of highly publicised media reports, and some academic studies discussing terrorist organisations plotting on the dark web (Ehney & Shorter, 2016; Weimann, 2015), hitmen for hire, so-called red rooms in which one can view the murder of another person and the sale of sex slaves. However, there remains no academic evidence attesting to the actual existence of these enterprises actually being, in Gehl's words, *legit* (Gehl, 2018, p. 26). It remains, as in the case of Besa Mafia, an alleged transnational hitman operation connected to organised crime

(Ormsby, 2016), highly likely that such sites are sophisticated scams preying on naiveté or merely morbid scams.

In addition to only being accessible through Tor, *Silk Road* only accepted Bitcoin as a method of payment. As discussed previously, the concept of digital cash dates back to the late 1980s (Chaum et al., 1988; Nakamoto, 2008). An important distinction is between *cash* and electronic payment methods like PayPal, credit cards and so forth: the latter all remain under centralised control, while the innovation of digital cash, in this case Bitcoin, is decentralisation. The lack of centralised control allowed for a degree of anonymity and the circumvention of intermediaries who could regulate the flow of currency (Böhme, Christin, Edelman, & Moore, 2015). As a practical example, following a civil lawsuit brought by four alleged victims of underage sex trafficking, in 2015 the website *Backpage*, which provided advertisements for sexual services, was cut off from using services provided by MasterCard and Visa after the two payment processing companies were perceived to have bowed to state government pressure and withdrew their payment services (Finn & Stalans, 2016). The problem of censorship was thus mitigated by only allowing the use of Bitcoin which had no central actors that *could* censor.

1.3.3. Introducing Governance: Dispute Resolution and Escrow

A major innovation, at least in the context of illicit online commerce, which Silk Road provided was an escrow and dispute resolution system (Christin, 2013, p. 214). Transaction failures and conflicts were sought, remedied or resolved through the use of a *dispute resolution* centre (Ormsby, 2014), in which marketplace moderators and administrators would seek to resolve conflicts (Morselli, Décary-Hétu, Paquet-Clouston, & Aldridge, 2017). Because of the escrow system, in which administrators would act as mediators holding on to funds until a buyer had reported the exchange as finalised, transaction failures (e.g. not receiving product) could be resolved with a refund paid to either the seller or buyer depending on who was judged at fault. While an innovation in the context of illicit online commerce, the system essentially reproduced the 'backdrop' (Granovetter, 2017, p. 69) of institutional guarantees or safeguards which exist in licit platform economies and online commerce in general (Décary-Hétu, Paquet-Clouston, & Aldridge, 2016). In these, transaction failures can be negotiated by involving moderators and administrators, or one can resort to credit card refunds, cancelling a payment (Berry, 2018). The latter is technically impossible with Bitcoin payments, due to their irreversibility (Böhme et al., 2015), but by introducing a mediator to the transaction who held the money in escrow and was able to release it once the transaction was completed to the satisfaction of both parties, buyers effectively gained the potential for recourse. The escrow and dispute resolution system, in particular, fascinated criminologists who traditionally approach illegal markets as existing in opposition to the state, and thus beyond the institutions that can control, regulate and sanction predatory and deviant behaviour (Beckert & Wehinger, 2013; Jacques & Wright, 2011). Yet, these systems sought to introduce something akin to courts in which breaches of contract or dishonesty could be resolved (Holt, Smirnova, Chua, & Copes, 2015; Moeller et al., 2017; Morselli et al., 2017). Importantly, similarly to licit platform economies, administrators held great power in this constellation of actors, since they could at will ban who they thought to be dishonest individuals, and had the final say in every ruling.

Yet, as Ormsby (2014) demonstrates, entrepreneurial scam artists were still capable of preying on others. The 'Great 420

Heist' in which the vendor *Tony76* convinced customers to finalise their transactions before they had received their product was estimated to have resulted in a theft from customers in the range of US$100,000–250,000 (Ormsby, 2014). The scam both proved both the futility, and the necessity, of the escrow and dispute resolution institution. On the one hand, predatory sellers could still 'game the system' and their methods of doing so have grown more sophisticated (Moeller et al., 2017), yet on the other, using escrow properly using escrow properly to avoid scams remained the best protection. scams remained the best protection.

1.3.4. Politics, Community and Book Clubs

Media attention proved a significant driver of Silk Road's popularity (Ormsby, 2014), and while drugs and technology were central to such attention, there remained a constant undercurrent of politics to this (Greenberg, 2013). Silk Road did not propose a party-based politics, but politics remained constantly looming in the background in a myriad of ways. A neat categorisation is not possible, but scholars have discussed the right-libertarian politics of Robert's and the community (Maddox, Barratt, Allen, & Lenton, 2016; Munksgaard & Demant, 2016; Zajácz, 2017; Zaunseder & Bancroft, 2019), an ethos of harm reduction (Barratt, Lenton, Maddox, & Allen, 2016; Van Hout & Bingham, 2013b; Van Hout & Hearne, 2017), opposition against the war on drugs (Ladegaard, 2017c) and remnants of a cipherpunk ethos (Bancroft & Scott Reid, 2017). Of course, none of these were incompatible.

In an interview given to Forbes (Greenberg, 2013), Dread Pirate Roberts discussed libertarian politics and how he saw *Silk Road* as a vehicle for state subversion through exchanges outside the purview of government, a peculiar brand of right-anarchist politics known as *agorism* (Munksgaard & Demant, 2016; Zaunseder & Bancroft, 2019). While running his growing empire, Robert's further organised a libertarian book club on the Silk Road forums where classical libertarian works would be discussed (Ormsby, 2014). As such, the exchange of drugs for Bitcoin on *Silk Road* took place in the shadow of a radical libertarian politics espoused by the platform's administration. The *Silk Road* forums also offered a place for discussing drugs, both in general and about specific substances (Van Hout & Bingham, 2013b). This wasn't entirely new as forums for discussing drug use, and the safe consumption of drugs, predate Silk Road but would typically be heavily moderated to avoid people trying to sell or buy drugs (Barratt, 2011).

It is important to not discount these forums, which over the years accrued thousands of posts wherein buyers and sellers would discuss both the practicalities of online drug dealing like shipping, plausible deniability and 'operational security' (aka 'OPSEC', the practice of securing oneself from detection by law enforcement). Such forums can function as archives for an abundance of knowledge, from methods of consumption and trip reports to the intense discussions within the community's early days (see, e.g., the studies by Bilgrei, 2016; Kamphausen & Werse, 2019; Ladegaard, 2017b; Van Hout & Hearne, 2017). For example, the Silk Road community heavily discussed both the sale of weapons, which Silk Road's franchise *The Armory* engaged in, and whether Silk Road should allow the sale of child sexual exploitation material.

1.3.5. 'This Hidden Site Has Been Seized'

From January 2011 to October 2013, Silk Road experienced growth that paralleled even the most 'disruptive' innovations.

Fig. 1.1. The Silk Road Seizure Banner which Greeted Visitors after 2 October 2013.

Source: https://commons.wikimedia.org/wiki/File:Silk_Road_Seized.jpg

Yet, despite the sophisticated technologies involved, the vehemently libertarian sentiment and unparalleled defiance, law enforcement still managed to identify the server, copy it, identify and arrest the administrator, Ross Ulbricht. It seemed that in a matter of days the entirety of what had been built in the preceding years had disappeared. However, Silk Road had provided a business model and nurtured both demand and supply, and law enforcement now inadvertently created a huge vacuum.

1.4. DOWNFALL OF A MONOPOLY

Throughout Silk Road's existence the demand for illicit drugs on the dark web had grown, and so had the population of vendors. At the same time, smaller competitors had launched platforms that were highly similar, namely Sheep Marketplace and Black Market Reloaded. Both utilised the Tor network, cryptocurrencies and the same platform infrastructure. Consequently, shortly after buyers and vendors had encountered the seizure notice they started migrating to these markets and in the span of one month Black Market Reloaded doubled its number of vendors, while Sheep Marketplace grew by 461% (Van Buskirk et al., 2014). Existing side by side with Silk Road, both were established and ready to absorb the now migratory population of buyers and vendors, but rapidly the ecosystem changed as a plethora of new markets began to launch, one of which, Silk Road 2.0, was a continuation of Silk Road with overlapping members in administrative positions. The period after the fall of Silk Road was one marked by chaos and rapid change: An influx of buyers and vendors (following the highly publicised fact that drugs could be bought online with relatively little risk), the existence of a large demand but no central platform, and a heightened discussion of how to solve a range of new problems that became apparent following the seizure, all marked this epoch.

1.4.1. Hacks, Scams and Chaos

Over the span of a few months several marketplaces were launched. In addition to Sheep Marketplace, Silk Road 2.0 and Black Market Reloaded, the two months after Silk Road saw the launch of Black Flag Project, TorMarket, Pandora, BlackBox Market, Dream Market, The Marketplace, Pirate Market, FloMarket, Black Services Market, Blue Sky, Agora, Tortuga, TorBay, White Rabbit and Outlaw Market, a trend which continued throughout 2014 (Branwen, 2015; Soska & Christin, 2015). Complicating the matter even further, the launch of new markets was followed by intra-market disputes and a free-for-all of hacker attacks, and worst of all, *the marketplace exit scam* (Moeller et al., 2017). All were new developments, and buyers and vendors thus had to adjust their expectations to a new normal.

The first intra-market dispute was seen when the administrator of Silk Road 2.0, who had revived the Dread Pirate Robert's moniker, hacked and leaked the database from their competitor TorMarket (Moeller et al., 2017). This was the final nail in their coffin following a period of downtime and unresponsiveness from administrators, and the market disappeared shortly after. Hackers and curious individuals simultaneously baptised every new market in fire, trying to find security vulnerabilities in markets or collect and publish *doxx*, that is, sensitive information, about the administrators (Branwen, 2015). Sheep Marketplace, for example, fell victim to the latter (DeepDotWeb, 2013a). As the administrator was arrested years later by Czech police, it turned out the doxx had been correct (DeepDotWeb, 2017b). FloMarket was hacked twice, and closed a month after its launch (Branwen, 2015).

The marketplace exit scam was however the most shocking development to the community and was analogous to, but bigger and more disruptive than, the vendor exit scam which Ormsby (2014) dissected in the case of Tony76. Because of the cryptomarket escrow system where all payments from pending transactions are held centrally, massive amount of funds amass on sites (Moeller et al., 2017). Since Bitcoin transactions are irreversible, once stolen the game is over and the money gone. With such a centralised system, administrators are the only ones with access to the funds and can abscond with every last Bitcoin at any time. The first massive exit scam was Sheep Marketplace, merely two months after the seizure of Silk Road and its sudden influx of buyers and vendors (DeepDotWeb, 2013a). Initially, the system for withdrawing Bitcoin from the site 'stopped working' while funds kept amassing. Even more suspicious and bizarre, the market administrators began to require a minimum of 1 bitcoin in an account for a user to be able to withdraw bitcoin, leading some users to deposit more bitcoin, in the hope of being able to withdraw what was in their account (DeepDotWeb, 2013b). By the end of November 2013, the game was up, and Sheep disappeared in the first major marketplace exit scam.[3] The most credible estimates of the exit scam suggest that around US$5 million were stolen from buyers and vendors (DeepDotWeb, 2017b).

There were obvious parallels between this chaotic period and the criminology of drug markets, but the format of these disputes, hacks and marketplace exit scams still differed significantly from the drug markets known to criminologists. Drug markets come in a variety of forms spanning the open street market to the closed social setting (Coomber & Moyle, 2014, 2017). Violence is not by default a component in drug markets, but often plays a significant role as a mode of conflict management, particularly in open-air markets (Jacques & Wright, 2008). While not violent in the physical sense, the marketplace exit scam mimics predatory and fraudulent behaviour in traditional drug markets, with one exception: Instead of victimising a single dealer or user, victimisation was 'global' in the sense that every vendor was defrauded. Moeller et al. (2017) argues that these behaviours constitute *fraudulent resource exchanges*, similar to 'rip-offs' in drug markets where, for example, a customer is hustled, cheated or otherwise subjected to fraud. While it might be possible to theorise the intra-market disputes, the fact remains that the attack on TorMarket has remained the only documented case that was 'successful' (i.e. caused major disruption).

From the seizure of Silk Road onwards the cryptomarket scene saw hacks, exit scams and new sites opening regularly.

Along with the trauma of Silk Road's seizure, a discussion of possible solutions became central within the community (Horton-Eddison & Di Cristofaro, 2017; Ladegaard, 2017a; Moeller et al., 2017). Thus, increasing risk from law enforcement and exit scams became central concerns. Marketplaces, of course, sought to capitalise on this and implemented new solutions. One cryptomarket, *The Marketplace*, took the lead by implementing multi-signature escrow and moving from the Tor network to the I2P network (Demant, Munksgaard, & Houborg, 2018). The move from Tor to I2P, a similar but still differently built anonymising network, was innovative and responded to a general scepticism towards the use of Tor. After all, Tor was in part funded by the US Government and it seemed as if the FBI was capable of shutting down websites making I2P a sensible alternative. The market is also credited with the first implementation of multi-signature escrow, an innovative solution to the problem of marketplace exit scams (Branwen, 2015): whereas in regular escrow, *centralised escrow*, funds remain under the absolute control of the mediator (i.e. the marketplace administration), multi-signature involves three keys. To finalise a transaction, two of three keys are needed. Thus, if the administration was to try and abscond with all funds, they would also need either the seller or buyer's key to release the funds (Kruithof et al., 2016). Sellers and buyers, however, could finalise the transaction without the involvement of the administration thus insulating them from the systemic risk imposed by the centralised escrow system.

Alongside these innovations, talk of *decentralised* cryptomarkets also grew. Glancing over the technical details, commentators and community members began pondering whether multi-signature escrow could feasibly be combined with a platform with no administrator. For a while, namely when activists in the cipherpunk spirit coded *DarkMarket*, a protocol for a decentralised cryptomarket (Greenberg, 2014), this seemed plausible. Yet, as 2014 continued reality did not conform to any of the hopes of decentralised cryptomarkets or multi-signature escrow and as time passed, cryptomarket buyers and vendors concentrated on three markets, Agora, Silk Road 2.0 and Evolution Marketplace – none of which offered multi-signature escrow (Branwen, 2015). In fact, due to an alleged hack in February 2014, Silk Road 2.0 operated without escrow at all until its demise (Moeller et al., 2017). With three dominant markets, all following the same paradigm of design and implementation, the centralisation of illicit activity, like during Silk Road, was repeating itself.

1.4.2. Fraudsters and Politics

Whereas the cryptomarket ecosystem did not change significantly on the surface throughout 2014, qualitatively two things transpired throughout 2014 which were noteworthy. First, a marked trend of *depoliticisation* took place, and second, despite some critical voices in the community, the cryptomarket economy slowly merged with the economy for stolen data.

Silk Road was launched under libertarian slogans of waging economic warfare against the state (Munksgaard & Demant, 2016), and the rules and regulations had a distinct libertarian ethos emphasising personal responsibility and not harming others. Silk Road 2.0, while launched under the same banner, never managed the same eloquence in their public posts, and most marketplace administrators refrained from political discussion. Measuring indicators of political discourse in cryptomarket forums, Munksgaard and Demant (2016) found that the closure of Silk Road coincided with the almost complete disappearance of politics as a topic of discussion. Alongside these two trends towards less political discussion and apolitical administrators, cryptomarkets slowly began altering their product selection beyond the strict limit of illicit substances and towards stolen data: hacking tools, credit card information, tutorials on fraud and so forth. The rise and success of Evolution Marketplace made this change apparent.

Evolution was launched in January 2014, and the two administrators, *Verto* and *Kimble*, were known figures in the cybercrime scene outside cryptomarkets (DeepDotWeb, 2015b). Before the launch of Evolution, Verto and Kimble had operated Tor Carding Forum, a forum dedicated to the 'carding' scene (i.e. the market for and community around the sale and use of stolen data). Whereas other cryptomarkets had dealt in similar goods, or were beginning to, Evolution had explicit and known ties to this community. Criticism was vocal, namely from the figure *the_avid* who had exposed insecurities in some of the new cryptomarkets. Against the increasing overlap, *the_avid* argued that the carding community was known for being on the radar of law enforcement and prone to infiltration by them, that administrators and moderators were unable to constrain fraudulent behaviour, and that platforms and users had low standards of operational security (DeepDotWeb, 2015b).

1.4.3. First as Tragedy, then as Farce (with Minor Adjustments)

As 2014 came towards its end, the cryptomarket ecosystem had survived the seizure of Silk Road, new markets had proliferated, and the economy had bounced back and grown. A marked trend of *depoliticisation*, at least on the surface, was apparent, and slowly cryptomarkets had begun to overlap with the market for stolen data. Yet, activity remained centralised on a few platforms which were essentially similar to the original Silk Road. One of them was even named Silk Road 2.0. The innovative solutions to marketplace exit scams and law enforcement operations, multi-signature, decentralised platforms and I2P, remained unadopted beyond the fringes of the ecosystem. In October 2014 history repeated itself, as Silk Road 2.0 was seized almost a year after its predecessor along with a handful of smaller cryptomarkets (Décary-Hétu & Giommoni, 2017; Soska & Christin, 2015). The old refrain, *first as tragedy, then as farce*, seemed appropriate as the conclusion to a chaotic 12 months was a near-repetition of what had happened nearly a year earlier.

1.5. ONYMOUS AND ONWARDS

Operation Onymous, which took place roughly a year after the seizure of Silk Road, was an international effort by law enforcement. Simultaneously, law enforcement seized servers and shut down a handful of markets, of which Silk Road 2.0 was the largest. The tendency of buyers and vendors to migrate to competing platforms following such intervention, as had happened in the wake of Silk Road, took place yet again (Décary-Hétu & Giommoni, 2017). Quickly, the two markets Agora and Evolution came to dominate the economy (Soska & Christin, 2015). This epoch, beginning with operation Onymous in 2014 and continuing to this day, is marked by a settlement of the patterns seen before. Throughout this period, depoliticisation, centralisation, and the overlap between the market for drugs and the market for fraud and stolen data, has become the norm.

With Tochka Marketplace, a medium-sized cryptomarket existing since 2015 being the only exception, the political ethos which distinguished Silk Road is generally no longer espoused by cryptomarket administrators. Similarly, the tendency for cryptomarkets to overlap with markets for stolen data has also settled. Most large cryptomarkets will offer products that relate to this economy, with some even implementing *autoshops*, interfaces for buying stolen data like credit card information. Alphabay, which at its seizure was the largest operating cryptomarket, had known ties to this economy, just like Evolution Marketplace (DeepDotWeb, 2015b, 2015c)

However, while the cryptomarket ecosystem in broad terms has, as we argue, *settled*, this epoch has still seen some changes of interest to scholars. While research on these subjects remains sparse, most cryptomarkets now allow payments in cryptocurrencies other than Bitcoin and geographically restricted markets have joined the ecosystem. We discuss the former, alternative currencies, in the final chapter as this is a development that has not been fully realised and lacks research, while we in this section treat the tendency towards centralisation and the increase in regional markets.

1.5.1. Centralisation

The migration to Evolution and Agora, of which neither offered new additions like multi-signature escrow, cemented a pattern which came to repeat itself in the cryptomarket economy: As one market ends, whether voluntarily through exit scamming or law enforcement intervention, buyers and vendors will migrate to competing markets (Décary-Hétu & Giommoni, 2017; Soska & Christin, 2015; Van Buskirk et al., 2017). While it remains unexamined in the literature, it seems that buyers and vendors will typically move to the second largest market. For example, after Evolution exit scammed, users migrated to Agora. This pattern of *centralisation* has become a marked quality of the cryptomarket ecosystem. Generally, there will at all times, except in the aftermath of a closure, be one or two markets on which most trade is concentrated (Décary-Hétu & Giommoni, 2017; Soska & Christin, 2015). Next to them, a handful of smaller markets with some activity will persist. Following a closure, users will then migrate to the best alternative out of the smaller markets, often the one with most activity. To ensure as stable a transition as possible, vendors may operate backup-accounts in the smaller markets, thus being able to rapidly guide their customers to their next preferred platform in case of an exit scam or law enforcement intervention (Soska & Christin, 2015).

Having become a regular pattern, law enforcement exploited the pattern of centralisation in 2016 after having seized the, at the time, largest cryptomarket, Alphabay (Greenberg, 2018). In June 2016, the seizure of Alphabay was announced, and the community began discussing alternate platforms on Reddit, DeepDotWeb and various cryptomarket forums. The cryptomarket Hansa Marketplace, which had operated for a while and gained a good reputation, became the primary choice, and over the coming weeks, buyers and vendors began using the market. Unbeknownst to them, however, law enforcement had both arrested the administrators of Hansa and gained control of the server. Thus, one of the worst-case scenarios that had always been discussed in the cryptomarket communities, the *honeypot* (Afilipoaie & Shortis, 2018) came to fruition: Dutch law enforcement had full access to the platform and communications on it. To 'maximize' the yield from their operation, Dutch law enforcement used some highly innovative techniques (Greenberg, 2018). First, posing as administrators they notified vendors that due to an error, they would have to re-upload product images. Image files can contain metadata such as geolocation or camera identifiers that not every vendor would be skilled enough to remove. Thus, law enforcement was now in possession of a trove of data from these sellers. Further proving their ingenuity, Dutch law enforcement performed a *man-in-the-middle* attack on the use of PGP keys. Inserting their own PGP key instead of the vendor's key, they acted as a middleman between buyer and vendor gaining access to tracking numbers and shipping addresses, despite buyers and vendors following best practice for encryption.

Nevertheless, following the seizure of both Hansa and Alphabay, Dream Marketplace grew into the largest market until its (apparent[4]) voluntary closure in 2019 (DeepDotWeb, 2019). Wall Street Market, one of Dream's competitors, seemed an ideal choice but following the influx and attention, the market absconded with all funds in escrow only to be seized by law enforcement days later (Cimpanu, 2019; Winder, 2019). As such, patterns of centralisation, exit scams and intervention came to repeat themselves in a now all too familiar manner.

1.5.2. Localisation

Throughout this and the second epoch, the traditionally international cryptomarket also began to expand into local platforms. As of today, local cryptomarkets catering to Brazil (Mercado Negro), Sweden (Flugsvamp, Flugsvamp 2.0), North America (Cannabis Growers' and Merchants' Cooperative), Britain (Rapture), France (French Deep Web Market), Italy (Berlusconi Market, Italian Deep Web Market), Finland (Silkkitie) and Russia and Eastern Europe (Hydra) have all operated or continue to do so. Generally, they remain small in size compared to behemoths like Dream or Alphabay, which cater to a global audience. However, they still provide a niche wherein vendors and buyers within the same country can meet and exchange. At a general level, utilising a domestic platform *could* lower the risk of buyers and vendors being caught in an 'international dragnet'. A domestic platform also provides benefits such as acting in a market using one's native language and limits the supply to vendors who operate from a known jurisdiction. An absolute separation between domestic/international cryptomarkets, however, is not entirely fruitful. Some markets may begin as domestic platforms, only to later branch out and 'go international', as was done by Silkkitie and Cannabis Growers' and Merchants' Cooperative (Nurmi, Kaskela, Perälä, & Oksanen, 2017).

1.5.3. Increasing and Novel External Action

Beginning with the seizure of Silk Road in 2013, disruptive interventions by law enforcement have remained a staple of the cryptomarket economy. Arrests of vendors, and sometimes buyers, remain a constant in the background with large-scale interventions occasionally interrupting the ecosystem: the seizure of Silk Road; the subsequent Operation Onymous; and later seizures of markets like Alphabay and Hansa Marketplace. Throughout the third epoch, however, law enforcement has adopted new strategies. We note a pattern of closing key nodes in the community and using what can best be described as scare tactics aimed at undermining institutional trust.

In the former category, we find the seizure of DeepDotWeb and subsequent arrests of the administrators (Caleb, 2019). For years, DeepDotWeb had functioned as an unofficial news organ for the community in which marketplace exit scams were reported, relevant news was published, and users could find links to cryptomarkets supplied by a trusted actor. The latter, however, had earned DeepDotWeb a significant amount of Bitcoin, since the links to the markets they provided would earn the administrators commission from buyers who followed them (i.e. 'referral links'). In a similar vein, though not enforced by law enforcement, Reddit closed the largest cryptomarket-related forum on the clear web, r/DarkNetMarkets, and a number of smaller forums following changes in content policy intended to curb illegal activity (Reddit Policy, 2018). In both cases, the key implication is the disappearance of nodes of information, both functioning as trusted news outlets as well as repositories of information dating back years (Aldridge, Stevens, & Barratt, 2018; Masson & Bancroft, 2018; Moeller et al., 2017). These locations provided users with information relevant to both the usage of cryptomarkets (e.g. how not to get scammed by vendors, how to use PGP) and a harm reduction resource (e.g. who supplies proper drugs). While a Reddit alternative, *Dread*, is operational on the dark web, it does not compare to the amount of information and activity provided by the Reddit forum.

In terms of law enforcement operations, a theme has emerged in recent operations that were not aimed solely at seizing markets which is best summed up as *the dark web is not as safe as you thought* – often referred to as 'spreading FUD' (fear, uncertainty and doubt) amongst members of the cryptomarket community. These operations aim to undermine the trust in the cryptomarket as an institution (Tzanetakis, 2018b), with the prime example being law enforcement operating Hansa Marketplace for a month while siphoning off data and exploiting PGP (Greenberg, 2018). Similarly, during Operation Hyperion (Cox, 2016; DeepDotWeb, 2017a), law enforcement agencies most likely exploited customer lists kept by vendors to knock on the doors of former buyers. These disruptions were followed by press releases stating that the 'clear message for people who think they can use the internet to buy illegal drugs and get away with it is that they can't' (New Zealand Police, 2016) and 'there is a misconception that the Darknet is a place to operate without any risk of police intervention' (RCMP, 2016). These statements are illustrative of an approach that seeks to undermine not only the markets themselves, but also the trust buyers place in markets, technology and vendors.

1.6. CONCLUSION

In reviewing the history of cryptomarkets, it becomes evident that *not much has changed since Silk Road*, in terms of organisation and technology. In fact, present-day cryptomarkets utilise the same structure, the same technologies and are organised in essentially the same way as Silk Road. Tzanetakis (2018b) discusses these similarities within the theoretical vocabulary of economic sociology, arguing that they are 'informal institutional standardisations' (Tzanetakis, 2018b, p. 76). The absence of organisational development since Silk Road is reflected in the similar introductory sections of most academic articles on this topic, which invariably allude to the origins of cryptomarkets being seen in Silk Road. Yet, while the cryptomarket has remained 'intact', other forms of illicit online markets have developed, namely drug distribution on social media like Facebook, which we return to in Chapter 4. In this chapter, we have treated the history of the cryptomarket arguing that Silk Road presented a new model for online drug distribution, which over the coming years began to 'settle'. Despite large-scale intervention from law enforcement, and predatory administrators periodically stealing from buyers and vendors, the ecosystem has shown itself to be highly resilient.

One way to approach the cryptomarket as a phenomenon is to consider it as a *social institution* (Tzanetakis, 2018b), a set of 'persistent patterns defining how some specified collection of social actions are and should be carried out'

(Granovetter, 2017, p. 136). From this perspective, the history outlined in this chapter is that of a website, *Silk Road*, which settled and became a persistent pattern organising the illicit trade of drugs in one domain. Illustrative of this, what we termed the second epoch saw a variety of innovative attempts at improving the cryptomarket: *Multi-signature escrow*, *decentralised markets*, the use of *I2P*, yet, none of these were widely adopted, and remained on the fringes of the cryptomarket ecosystem. Thus, despite innovations and a plethora of new markets, a stable pattern emerged. This pattern encompasses the use of cryptocurrencies, namely Bitcoin, the escrow system and the use of Tor which have all been a component of cryptomarkets, and for which the utilisation has hardly changed since Silk Road (Martin, 2014a, 2014b). In other words, Silk Road provided a formula which became the standard. In taking this approach, however, the historical, political and social legacy of cryptomarkets should not be ignored: Silk Road did not emerge in a vacuum. Rather, it innovated *within* an already existing online drug economy by introducing a platform design in combination with politically invested technologies for encryption and anonymity.

NOTES

1. The odd choice of words by the administrator, Dread Pirate Roberts, during the interview was because he referenced a previous administrator. Whether Ross Ulbricht, the man behind the pseudonym, was speaking the truth or trying to cover his tracks, the fact remains that he was sentenced for being the only administrator.

2. Some later cryptomarkets required 'invites', invitation links. However, these were rarely hard to come by and easily found through a simple web search. In many cases, the inviter would earn a commission on invitees who used their links. Consequently, these

invitations are hardly comparable to those required by hacker and fraud forums, documented by Dupont et al. (2017) and Holt et al. (2018) and more likely functioned as marketing.

3. We note that information was revealed during the trial against the administrator of Sheep Marketplace, which suggests that the exit scam was provoked by an outside theft (DeepDotWeb, 2017b).

4. At the time of writing, it is not entirely clear what happened to Dream Market, and voluntary closure is what we consider the most likely reason.

2

THE CURRENT STATE OF THE CRYPTOMARKET TRADE

2.1. THE STATE OF CRYPTOMARKETS

Building upon the historical narrative offered in Chapter 1, this chapter is intended to provide a detailed and up-to-date overview of the current state of cryptomarkets. We discuss the size, scope and composition of cryptomarkets, with a particular focus on their commonalities and shared characteristics, including their developmental phases, prohibitions of different goods and services, regional variations and the mechanisms underpinning them, and their collective impact upon transnational drug trafficking networks. The methodologies underpinning the research used below will be the focus of the following chapter.

2.1.1. Overall Market Size and Growth

As detailed in Chapter 1, from their modest beginnings in 2011, cryptomarkets have experienced a steady upward trajectory in terms of growth. Since that time, estimated trading frequencies, product listings, revenues, and the number of cryptomarkets, buyers and vendors in operation have all increased, notwithstanding temporary disruptions due to law enforcement takedowns or market-level exit scams, the effects of which will be explored later in the chapter. In terms of overall trends regarding the size of the cryptomarket-facilitated illicit drug trade, in early 2013 estimates for the gross annual turnover of *Silk Road*, which had a near monopoly on the cryptomarket drug trade at that time, range between US$90 (Aldridge & Décary-Hétu, 2014) and US$100 million per annum (Soska & Christin, 2015). By 2015, total revenues for the eight largest cryptomarkets in operation were estimated at US$25 million per month (Kruithof et al., 2016) which, if extrapolated out to an annual figure, suggests an overall revenue in the order of US$350 million, more than a tripling of the size of the market in just three years. While there have been no studies examining the overall size of the cryptomarket trade published since 2016, individual market studies, such as Tzanetakis' (2018a) analysis of *Alphabay*, suggest continued growth, with the revenue of this single cryptomarket estimated at US$94 million in the year up to August 2016.

Despite the remarkable and ongoing growth of the cryptomarket drugs trade, it comprises only a tiny percentage of the global illicit drugs trade as a whole. Estimates of the total size and associated revenues of the worldwide trade in illicit drugs are wildly variable and notoriously rife with methodological difficulties and problematic assumptions (Reuter & Greenfield, 2001).[1] Notwithstanding these limitations, the total value of the worldwide trade in illicit drugs is estimated to be in the order of US$426–652 billion per annum (May, 2017). If accurate, these figures suggest that cryptomarkets account for less than 0.1% of the total global trade in illicit drugs. However, given their steady growth, it appears likely that an increasing proportion of the overall drugs trade is shifting to cryptomarkets, at least in those countries in North America, Europe and Oceania in which rates of cryptomarket usage are the highest (Demant, Munksgaard, Décary-Hétu, & Aldridge, 2018; Dittus, Wright, Graham., 2017; Dolliver & Kenney, 2016; Martin, Cunliffe, Décary-Hétu, & Aldridge, 2018b).

At present, the steady growth of the cryptomarket-facilitated drugs trade appears almost certain to continue. This is because the factors that are underpinning this growth are largely stable. These factors include the widespread demand for illicit goods and services, particularly drugs, and the persistence of the global regime of drug prohibition that, notwithstanding some significant changes concerning cannabis regulation in North America, has created the regulatory vacuum that drives and sustains one of the largest black markets ever witnessed (May, 2017). Also critical to the continued growth of cryptomarkets is the censorship-resistant properties of the tools and technologies used for anonymisation and encryption, namely Tor and cryptocurrencies. Despite some periodic but significant successes on the part of law enforcement in taking down some cryptomarkets and de-anonymising cryptomarket traders (see Section 1.5), the strength of investigative tools appears limited and does not currently pose a credible threat to the market ecosystem (Décary-Hétu & Giommoni, 2017; Ladegaard, 2019). In short, while individual cryptomarkets and vendors have come and gone, the system as a whole remains resilient and looks set for continued growth.

An additional factor driving the expansion of cryptomarkets is their attractiveness to both buyers and sellers of illicit drugs. Data from the Global Drug Survey (GDS, 2018) indicate that the proportion of drug consumers worldwide who have purchased drugs from cryptomarkets has risen from 4.7% in 2014 to 9.3% in 2018. While these numbers are likely to be an over-estimate due to the methodological biases inherent to the GDS (as discussed in Section 4.3.3), the trend towards steady growth remains clear. For buyers, cryptomarkets present several advantages over in-person forms of drug exchange. These advantages include cheaper prices, greater variety and increased purity, or at least perceptions of purity, of drugs that are sourced via other means (Caudevilla et al., 2016; Van Buskirk, Roxburgh et al., 2016). A further advantage offered by cryptomarkets, one that is relevant to both buyers and vendors, is the reduced risk of violence, which is a central characteristic of cryptomarket-facilitated drug exchanges in which buyers and sellers never meet in person (Barratt, Ferris, & Winstock, 2016; Martin, 2014a, 2014b). While threats and other forms of digital harassment and exploitation such as doxing, fraud and predation between buyers and vendors do sometimes occur (Moeller et al., 2017; Morselli et al., 2017), such instances are relatively uncommon, with online dispute resolution mechanisms and public reputation systems serving to maintain a largely peaceful trading environment.

2.1.2. Cryptomarket Lifecycle

While the cryptomarket ecosystem as a whole has proven remarkably resilient, growing and diversifying steadily since the launch of *Silk Road* in 2011, individual cryptomarkets remain highly vulnerable and are typically operational for only a short period of time. In a review of 87 cryptomarkets between 2012 and 2017, Branwen (2017)[2] finds that more than 80% shut down within their first twelve months of operation, and that approximately 60% go offline in fewer than six months. Despite the high turnover and short period of operations associated with most cryptomarkets, a number of different stages of development – which collectively we term the *cryptomarket lifecycle* – are identifiable. We separate these into four stages: comprising infancy, adolescence, maturity and death. The first three of these stages are not intended to represent a discrete empirical reality, but rather a taxonomy through which one can identify general characteristics that change over time as cryptomarkets flow from one stage to the next. The time periods associated with the first three stages are similarly intended as a rough guide and are not prescriptive. By contrast, death, the final stage in the cryptomarket lifecycle, represents a discrete and conclusive end state, the causes of which are discussed following the overview of the different developmental stages presented below.

Infancy (up to six months): This is the first developmental phase in the cryptomarket lifecycle and is characterised by an initial launch, where market administrators bring their cryptomarket online and seek to publicise their new enterprise in order to attract vendors and customers. Launches are typically associated with marketing activity, such as interviews on clear web sites such as the (now defunct) *DeepDotWeb.com* (see, e.g., DeepDotWeb, 2015a, 2016a, 2016b). In these fora, market administrators are able to discuss their business philosophy, as well as market innovations that differentiate their site from its competitors. Infancy is the riskiest stage of the cryptomarket lifecycle as fledgling sites become exposed to the various threats that abound in the market ecosystem.

Adolescence (6–8 months): The adolescent phase is characterised by modest growth as well as a developing stability in market operations. In this stage, administrators seek to establish their bona fides amongst the wider cryptomarket community and generate trust in their platform in anticipation of an opening in the more mature (and profitable) upper segments of the market ecosystem. Adolescence is also the phase at which vendors with a presence on mature cryptomarkets may begin to diversify and establish back up profiles on adolescent cryptomarkets, which may be used in the event that their main trading platform is taken offline. Adolescent cryptomarkets therefore play an important role in the ongoing stability of the cryptomarket ecosystem as they represent the next generation of viable trading platforms to which vendors and customers will migrate in the inevitable event that mature cryptomarkets are taken offline (Martin, 2014a; Norbutas, 2018; van Wegberg & Verburgh, 2018).

Maturity (18+ months): Maturity is the stage at which cryptomarkets realise their greatest potential in terms of overall size and profitability and establish their position at the apex of the cryptomarket ecosystem. On current trends, it appears that there are typically 1–2, and likely no more than 4 mature cryptomarkets in operation at any one time (Soska & Christin, 2015). These mature sites comprise a monopoly or oligopoly which dominates the cryptomarket drugs trade (Tzanetakis, 2018b). Classic examples of this mono/oligopolistic market structure in recent years, also discussed previously in Chapter 1, include: Silk Road; Sheep Marketplace and Black Market Reloaded; and Silk Road 2, Agora and Evolution.

Few cryptomarkets survive to maturity, with Branwen (2017) showing that just 13% of cryptomarkets remain online past 18 months. Perhaps a more important indicator of cryptomarket maturity than longevity, however, is size relative to competitors. During periods of market instability when there are multiple closures of mature cryptomarkets, the length of time necessary to achieving a dominant position relative to competitors becomes shorter. For example, following Operation Onymous, where multiple mature cryptomarkets were simultaneously taken down by law enforcement, the cryptomarket Evolution was propelled into maturity after just 10 months online (Décary-Hétu & Giommoni, 2017). If a cryptomarket does make it to maturity, the rewards are great, as it is these dominant sites that make up the greatest proportion of cryptomarket drug sales (Soska & Christin, 2015) as vendors and customers alike are attracted to the institutional trust that market administrators have established over the lifecycle of the site. This prominence comes at a cost, however, as law enforcement agencies step up investigations into those sites which are responsible for the majority of cryptomarket-facilitated drug transactions.

Death: Cryptomarket closures are the result of at least one of four catastrophic processes. These are, in order of likelihood: exit scam, voluntary exit, hack by an external party, and take down by law enforcement (Branwen, 2017; Moeller et al., 2017). As discussed in Chapter 1, *Exit scams* occur when the administrator of a cryptomarket voluntarily closes their site, but does not warn traders in advance and instead absconds with funds that have been stored in user escrow accounts. Exit scams are the most common cause of cryptomarket mortality, accounting for approximately 45% of site closures. The risk of exit scams peaks in the middle stages of cryptomarket development, and accounting for 65% of closures in the adolescent stage (Branwen, 2017). The reasons for this trend are currently unclear, though a logical supposition is that administrators of adolescent cryptomarkets have sufficient funds available in user escrow accounts as to incentivise defrauding their patrons while the 'going is good' and attention from law enforcement is still low (Zaunseder & Bancroft, 2019).

Given their prevalence, exit scams are now accepted as an unfortunate but anticipated ending for most cryptomarkets (Tzanetakis, Kamphausen, Werse, & von Laufenberg, 2016). Unlike other modes of mortality, however, exit scams attract the ire of the cryptomarket community, and threats of violence and doxxing – whereby identifiable information about users (in this case, market administrators) is released publicly – are often made by traders who have been defrauded.

A notable example in this regard is the exit scam perpetrated by the administrators of Evolution, which resulted in the theft of between US$10 and US$15 million in Bitcoin from user escrow accounts, and prompted angry traders to post a 'bounty' on information that could be used to publicly identify those responsible (Tzanetakis et al., 2016). It appears that the chances of successfully executing an exit scam (i.e. absconding with user funds and remaining unidentified) are relatively high, with few cases of market administrators either being caught by law enforcement or publicly identified.

Voluntary exit refers to when market administrators make the decision to take their cryptomarket offline but, unlike when executing an exit scam, instead forewarn traders of the site's imminent closure, allowing sufficient time for users to fulfil outstanding orders and withdraw funds held in escrow accounts. Voluntary exits account for just over 30% of all cryptomarket closures, with prominent examples including *Agora* and *Dream Market*. Voluntary exists are the leading cause of mortality amongst infant cryptomarkets, accounting for 40% closures at this early stage of development (Branwen, 2017). Again, at present, the reasons for this are not known, though one may plausibly speculate that administrators of infant cryptomarkets, newly aware of the risks with which they are faced, may wish to 'honourably' exit the scene without damaging the trust placed in them by traders, or perhaps less altruistically, without risking stealing from members of the cryptomarket community who are willing to place a bounty on their heads. Because the trust between market administrators and traders is kept intact, voluntary exits represent the least disruptive of market closures, allowing ample time for buyers and sellers to conclude their affairs before migrating peacefully to an alternative site.

Hacks by external parties involve the penetration of a cryptomarket with the intention of stealing user data and/or cryptocurrencies stored in user escrow accounts. Branwen (2017) identifies 28 publicly known successful hacks targeting cryptomarkets between 2011 and 2017, with the majority of the attacks targeting infant cryptomarkets. Thirteen of the hacks identified by Branwen (2017) proved fatal, with 11 resulting in the closure of infant cryptomarkets. These figures suggest that while external hacks can occur at all stages of the cryptomarket lifecycle, they are disproportionately targeted at infant cryptomarkets and, in the event that they successfully penetrate the site, are most likely to cause lethal damage when they occur at this early stage. Hacks are particularly dangerous during infancy because new cryptomarkets are less likely to have robust security, and do not have sufficient institutional trust and financial liquidity to survive the loss of user data and funds in the event that a hack is successful. More mature cryptomarkets, by contrast, are likely to have more advanced security measures, as well as both greater financial and reputational resources that are necessary to recover from a successful hack.

The hacking attacks that targeted the mature cryptomarket *Silk Road 2.0* and infant the cryptomarket *Cannabis Road* provide a useful example of the variable levels of resilience cryptomarkets have to external hacks depending upon their stage of development. In February 2015, *Silk Road 2.0* became victim of an external hack[3] which resulted in the theft of approximately US$2.6 million worth of user funds (Rizzo, 2014b). Despite this loss, the site was able to recover and continue functioning, with administrators eventually providing compensation to an estimated 80% of users affected by the hack. *Cannabis Road*, by contrast, after only four months in operation, was hit with an external hack which resulted in the theft of approximately US$100,000. Despite the comparatively small value of funds lost, this effectively wiped out all of the funds stored by the site administrators who, unable to offer a realistic plan to compensate their customers, had no choice but to close the site (Rizzo, 2014a).

Law enforcement take downs are the least likely cause of cryptomarket closure, accounting for less than 15% of site closures, and most commonly affecting cryptomarkets at later stages of development (Branwen, 2017). The reasons for this are clear: cryptomarkets that are in operation for longer periods of time, and that are responsible for the largest proportion of illicit transactions inevitably become the highest priority targets for law enforcement, and therefore have the greatest amount of investigative resources dedicated to their closure. Infant cryptomarkets, by contrast, make less attractive targets, not only because they are smaller, but also because their higher rates of mortality due to other causes means that most will be taken offline without law enforcement intervention. Law enforcement take downs typically produce a limited impact on the cryptomarket ecosystem. While a takedown may produce a temporary disruption, traders are typically quick to adapt, migrating to alternative cryptomarkets and resuming normal operations in a short span of time (Décary-Hétu & Giommoni, 2017; Van Buskirk et al., 2017).

2.1.3. Geographical Distribution and Regional Clustering

Early cryptomarket studies highlighted their potential to transcend the boundaries of geography, and to facilitate a vast, globally integrated network of drug exchange connecting previously 'geographically and culturally disparate drug markets' (Martin, 2014a). To some extent, these early predictions have proven true; cryptomarkets have provided a unique platform whereby buyers and sellers located all over the world can meet and trade drugs in the one digital location and they have the potential (at least) to also catalyse the development of novel drug distribution networks that stretch across all continents (Aldridge & Décary-Hétu, 2015; Demant, Munksgaard, et al., 2018).

However, while they are online phenomena, and therefore inherently transnational in nature, it is becoming increasingly apparent that the cryptomarket economy is embedded, shaped and structured by the national and multi-national customs jurisdictions, economies, and drug markets within which vendors and consumers are physically embedded. This section will discuss these themes, exploring the regional nuances and variations inherent to the cryptomarket drugs trade, including different regional trends and characteristics of cryptomarket usage, as well as how and why geographical separation both enables and inhibits different forms of cryptomarket drug exchange.

The nature and extent of cryptomarket usage varies markedly depending upon where in the world one is located. As noted previously in the chapter, the majority of the cryptomarket drugs trade is concentrated in North America, Europe and Australia, countries which are typically associated with the Global North (Cunliffe, Martin, Décary-Hétu, & Aldridge, 2017; Dittus et al., 2017; Martin et al., 2018b; Norbutas, 2018; Van Buskirk, Naicker, Roxburgh, Bruno, & Burns, 2016). By contrast, traders – either buyers or sellers – are conspicuously absent from the Global South, with almost no buying or selling taking place in most countries in Asia, Africa and South America. However, even within active trading regions in the Global North, there are significant regional variations in terms of the rates of the overall numbers of buyers and sellers; rates of cryptomarket usage by drug users and suppliers relative to the size of the national population; the frequency with which they engage in cryptomarket trading;

and whether this trading activity is predominantly domestic, regional (i.e. concentrated within a particular continent), or supra-regional (i.e. between continents).

Multiple studies find the largest vendor population to be located in the US, while the European scene is dominated by the UK, Netherlands and Germany (Demant, Munksgaard, Décary-Hétu, et al., 2018; Kruithof et al., 2016; Martin et al., 2018b; Tzanetakis, 2018a). According to Cunliffe et al. (2017), in 2016, there were just over 2,000 cryptomarket drug vendors operating worldwide, with 38.1% located in Europe, 35.5% in North America, 7.4% in Australia and 1.5% in Asia (17.5% of vendors did not disclose their location). European vendors accounted for half (50.1%) of the all of transactions recorded on cryptomarkets, North American vendors 34.5%, Australian vendors 6.7%, and Asian vendors just 0.6% (Cunliffe et al., 2017). In terms of overall numbers, the US is home to the greatest number of cryptomarket vendors (644), followed by the UK (265), Germany (163), the Netherlands (152), Australia (150) and Canada (97) (Martin et al., 2018b). In terms of rates of cryptomarket usage by drug users, according to the generalisability-limited data from the 2018 GDS, the proportion of drug users who made purchases via a cryptomarket is highest in Finland (45.8%), followed by England (24.6%), the US (18.1%), Australia (17.2%), Scotland (16.3%), Canada (9.7%) and Germany (7.4%) – though it should be strongly noted that these findings could be related to data collections procedure as noted in Section 3.3.3.

With cryptomarket trading activity concentrated almost entirely in the Global North, in countries which collectively account for just 7% of the world's population (Dittus et al., 2017), the North-South divide represents the most obviously apparent check on the 'global' pretensions of the cryptomarket drugs trade. Further undermining the global dimension of the cryptomarket trade is the fact that drug prices offered by cryptomarket vendors in different regions display considerably variability, which belies the convergence one would expect if these geographically disparate markets were highly integrated. For example, in their analysis of the Australian cryptomarket drugs trade, Cunliffe et al. (2017) find drug prices offered by domestic vendors are significantly higher than their foreign counterparts, reflecting the relationship between the local cryptomarket trade within the broader (expensive) Australian illicit drug market – a discussion that will be returned to in Section 3.4.2. A majority of vendors in several high-usage cryptomarket countries, particularly Australia and the US also restrict their sales to domestic customers only (Cunliffe et al., 2017; Martin et al., 2018b). Even more revealing is recent international research that demonstrates that cryptomarket transactions predominantly take place between buyers and sellers who are either located in the same country or are within regional trading zones, particularly the European Union (Demant, Munksgaard, Décary-Hétu, et al., 2018; Norbutas, 2018). This trend towards localisation also appears to be increasing over time, with a diminishing proportion of cryptomarket transactions occurring across national borders despite an overall increase in the number of vendors and consumers worldwide (Demant, Munksgaard, Décary-Hétu, et al., 2018).

At first glance, this situation appears puzzling. Rates of illicit drug usage are relatively high amongst many nations that are not represented on cryptomarkets (e.g. Egypt, Kazakhstan, Peacock et al., 2018), suggesting the potential for large, and as yet untapped customer bases. Also puzzling is that many countries that are well known as major sources of either production or transit for the global illicit drugs trade (e.g. Afghanistan, Columbia, Mexico; UNODC, 2018) are also largely absent from cryptomarkets. This begs the obvious questions: why are drug consumers located in the Global South not purchasing drugs on cryptomarkets? Why are drug suppliers located in these countries not using cryptomarkets to sell directly to consumers both domestically and internationally, particularly when the large differences in prices between traditional source and consumption countries would appear to offer a great incentive for such trade? And why is international cryptomarket trading within the Global North on the decline when the popularity of cryptomarkets appears to be steadily increasing in these regions?

The existing literature suggests that at least part of the answer to the first two of these questions appears to be a lack of access to necessary technological infrastructure, particularly access to the internet. In order to successfully use a cryptomarket, drug users first need reliable access to, as well as sufficient familiarity with the internet and associated technologies, namely Tor and PGP, as well as cryptocurrencies (Kowalski, Hooker, & Barratt, 2019; Martin, 2014a). It therefore follows that in countries where access to the internet is limited, so too is the usage of cryptomarkets for both the purchase and sale of illicit drugs. Indeed, when comparing different national rates of cryptomarket usage we see a broad positive correspondence with rates of internet access (Union, 2013). Unfamiliarity with English – the dominant language on most cryptomarkets – is a potential additional obstacle that limits drug suppliers in most traditional source countries using cryptomarket to sell to customers in foreign locations, although the growth of non-English language cryptomarkets that cater exclusively for specific national markets, notably in Central and Eastern Europe (Dark.fail, 2019), suggests that language obstacles can be overcome, at least in those countries with sufficiently high levels of internet usage to make cryptomarket usage feasible in the first instance.

While a lack of access to internet technology may explain the absence of cryptomarket trading in countries in the Global South, what factors explain the relatively low, and decreasing levels of integration between those national and regional drug markets that exhibit high levels of cryptomarket usage? Researchers offer at least four complementary explanations for this phenomenon. These include a preference amongst consumers to source drugs from domestic vendors due to: (1) increased risk of postal interception as drugs cross national borders (Aldridge & Askew, 2017; Martin, 2014b; Van Buskirk, Naicker, et al., 2016); and (2) reduced waiting times for drug consignments, which results in both greater convenience, as well as lower levels of stress experienced by buyers who may be worried that their package has been intercepted while in transit (Cunliffe et al., 2017). A third explanation is that vendors are also averse to the risks associated with sending drugs across international borders (Décary-Hétu et al., 2016; Demant, Munksgaard, Décary-Hétu, et al., 2018), which are typically much more heavily policed than domestic postal systems and may therefore result in lengthy delays and increased numbers of consignments intercepted. While the risk of arrest remains low for vendors who ship drugs internationally, Décary-Hétu et al. (2016) suggest that vendors are also sensitive to the risk of damage to their online reputation that results from packages that do not make it successfully to customers. Finally, the trend away from global integration may be explained by the growing number of vendors in cryptomarket using countries offering a wider variety of drugs to domestic customers. The growing presence of these vendors reduces the necessity for customers to take the risk of sourcing the drugs they want internationally in favour of 'going local' (Aldridge & Askew, 2017; Demant, Munksgaard, Décary-Hétu, et al., 2018).

2.1.4. Competition, Reputation and Sales

As discussed in Section 1.3.1, cryptomarkets distinguish themselves from other illicit online markets through their platform organisation wherein buyers can peruse the goods sold by all vendors, an atypical scenario in the context of drug markets in which goods are often sold within close social networks or limited geographical space (Aldridge & Décary-Hétu, 2016; Coomber & Moyle, 2014). However, a range of problems associated with illegal markets remain despite this organisation (Bakken et al., 2018; Beckert & Dewey, 2017; Beckert & Wehinger, 2013). Most prominently, there exists an asymmetrical distribution of information about product quality (Akerlof, 1970; Herley & Florêncio, 2010), and drugs, an *unstandardised* product of unknown quality, is exchanged for a currency which is standardised (Fanselow, 1990). Of course, any transaction takes place in the shadow of potential dishonesty, as a vendor may always renege on their promises and scam the buyer (Moeller et al., 2017). Consequently, questions such as *who* to trade with or *what* to pay become of interest, both of which are intrinsically linked to the implications of product illegality.

From the perspective of drug market economics, Paquet-Clouston, Décary-Hétu, & Morselli (2018) follow Reuter and Kleiman's (1986) argument that the constraints of product illegality shape drug markets by studying competition on the cryptomarket Alphabay. The authors find that a majority of vendors (around 90%) make very few to no sales whatsoever and are effectively spectators to the market combining to represent just 16% of overall sales made through the site. Nine percentage of vendors achieve a modicum of successful sales who between them account for 36% share of the market, while the remaining 1%, represented by just 25 vendors, accounted for 49% of all sales during the study period. These findings are supported by Soska and Christin (2015), who observe a similar pattern of a select few vendors undertaking a disproportionately large share of market transactions. Paquet-Clouston et al. (2018) further find that most vendors are specialised within specific drug categories, and this is the same independent of the level of success that a vendor enjoys, though high-level vendors tend to have more listings than the medium level, who in turn list more products than low-level vendors. Paquet-Clouston et al. (2018) further observed that sellers on average only remained active for a few months, a finding which is corroborated by Nurmi et al. (2017) and Soska and Christin (2015). In combination, these findings suggest that the market for drugs on cryptomarkets is both highly competitive, stratified and in flux, corresponding surprisingly well with Reuter's (1983) original analysis (Paquet-Clouston et al., 2018, p. 96).

A handful of studies have analysed the factors associated with the financial success of vendors focussing namely on its association with a vendor's performance in the reputation system (e.g. their average rating, the number of negative or positive ratings). Hardy and Norgaard (2015) were the first to find an association between reputation and a vendor's success in the cryptomarket context, and later their findings have been supported by Nurmi et al. (2017), Przepiorka et al. (2017) and Espinosa (2019). Broadly, scholars find that an increase in the number of positive ratings is associated with both a higher price-per-unit (e.g. gram of cannabis, dose of LSD) and a higher number of sales. These findings correspond to studies of reputation systems on the clear web (e.g. eBay), suggesting some broad equivalence between the micro-economics of both licit and illicit markets organised like platforms (Diekmann, Jann, Przepiorka, & Wehrli, 2014; Przepiorka, 2013; Przepiorka et al., 2017; Tadelis, 2016). However, behaviour is not entirely driven by reputation, as both Décary-Hétu and Quessy-Doré (2017) and Duxbury and Haynie (2018) find the transactional ties buyers establish with vendors to be predictive of economic action. Specifically, Décary-Hétu and Quessy-Doré (2017) find that buyers are loyal to sellers, while Duxbury and Haynie (2018) find that buyers returning to vendors seem to put less weight on reputation scores.

When considered from the perspective of a prospective customer, these market dynamics make sense. Given the competitive trading environment on cryptomarkets, customers are faced with an unprecedented burden of choice in deciding which vendors will receive their patronage (Paquet-Clouston et al., 2018, p. 90). In this environment, customers are attracted not only to vendors who offer competitively priced products, but also to those who appear 'trustworthy'. Vendors establish their bona fides through the display of detailed information about themselves and their products and a demonstrated track record of success through past customer feedback (Décary-Hétu & Quessy-Doré, 2017; Hardy & Norgaard, 2015; Przepiorka et al., 2017; Van Hout & Bingham, 2013a). Of course, the labour involved in reviewing profiles and comparing reputation scores can also be reduced by relying on personal experience (Granovetter, 1985, p. 490). These dynamics may well be mutually reinforcing, so that the top-performing 1% which accrues reputational capital is the primary choice of vendor for a new buyer, who then becomes a loyal return customer (Décary-Hétu & Quessy-Doré, 2017), thereby helping to keep the vendor in the 1%.

2.2. WHAT IS, AND IS NOT, ON CRYPTOMARKETS?

2.2.1. Market Composition, Demand and Supply

Of the various goods and services traded on cryptomarkets, illicit drugs are by far the most prominent, and make up the overwhelming majority of individual transactions as well as revenues that are subsequently generated (Demant, Munksgaard, Décary-Hétu, et al., 2018; Kruithof et al., 2016; Soska & Christin, 2015; Tzanetakis, 2018a). This section will focus on the composition of the various illicit drugs traded on cryptomarkets, with the following sections addressing the smaller sub-markets for non-drug goods and services, as well as weapons.

The cryptomarket drugs trade is embedded within broader illicit drug markets, and the composition of drugs sold thereon may be interpreted as reflecting some of the general usage patterns of drug using populations in those countries in which cryptomarket usage is most prevalent. Given that the majority of cryptomarket trading is concentrated in North America, Western Europe and Australia (Martin et al., 2018b; Soska & Christin, 2015), we would therefore expect that the demand for illicit drugs on cryptomarkets is influenced by the general demand and usage patterns in these particular regions. This is not to say that cryptomarket drug trading should exactly mirror general patterns drug usage; there are a range of factors that preclude this, with consumers who use cryptomarkets differentiated from the remainder of the drug using population by a range of factors, including access to and familiarity with computers, Tor and cryptocurrencies, as well as demographic variables such as age, education levels and so on (Van Buskirk, Roxburgh, et al., 2016).

With this caveat in mind, when examining the market composition of illicit drugs most popularly traded on cryptomarkets, the general correspondence between broader patterns of illicit drug demand and usage and cryptomarket supply becomes clear. For example, numerous papers all show that the six most popular drugs traded on cryptomarkets are cannabis, MDMA, prescription drugs, stimulants, psychedelics and opioids (Demant, Munksgaard, Décary-Hétu, et al., 2018;

Table 2.1. Cryptomarket Drug Composition from Soska and Christin (2015).

Drug Type	Percentage of Transactions
Cannabis	36
MDMA (ecstasy)	21
Prescription drugs	17
Stimulants	9
Psychedelics	5
Opioids	4

Kruithof et al., 2016; Martin et al., 2018b; Soska & Christin, 2015; Tzanetakis, 2018a). Data from the UNODC (2017, 2018) indicate that the drug usage rates in countries that have a significant presence on cryptomarkets broadly correspond to the popularity of drugs traded on cryptomarkets, with cannabis being the most popularly used drug in these respective regions, as well as correspondingly high usage rates for MDMA, prescription drugs and stimulants (see also Burns, Roxburgh, Bruno, & Van Buskirk, 2014; Cunliffe, Décary-Hétu, & Pollak, 2019; Van Buskirk, Naicker, et al., 2016).

The correspondence between cryptomarket drug sales and general usage patterns is somewhat surprising given that cryptomarkets offer consumers a much wider range of illicit drugs than is available from other sources of supply. This prospect has led some in the media and academia to speculate that the emergence of cryptomarkets has 'the potential to kickstart changes in the patterns and prevalence of drug use in the locations they are sold' (Aldridge & Décary-Hétu 2016, p. 12). While this may indeed be the case, there is currently insufficient evidence to suggest that the widespread availability of different kinds of drugs on cryptomarkets is causing major shifts in drug usage patterns. NPS, for example, are widely available on cryptomarkets, yet despite this they remain one of the least popularly traded categories of drugs across much of the world (Broséus et al., 2016; Martin et al., 2018b), though there is some evidence that growing numbers of cryptomarket vendors are at least offering these products for sale, particularly in the US and China (Van Buskirk, Naicker, et al., 2016). For the time being, however, it appears as though 'the most commonly sold substances on cryptomarkets are also those most commonly used among sentinel groups of people who use drugs' (Van Buskirk et al., 2016, 2017). This is particularly noteworthy since the sale of NPS was the predominant type of drug trade online before cryptomarkets (see Section 1.2).

The general mirroring of cryptomarket drug supply with general consumer demand suggests that cryptomarkets are largely reacting to existing market demands rather than altering them; that is, cryptomarket drug supply emerges in *response* to consumer demand, rather than the other way around (see also Dittus, Wright, & Graham, 2017). This pattern of demand leading supply is further evidenced by a study of the US opioid market conducted by Martin et al. (2018a). This study was prompted by a significant, unexplained and sustained increase in the trading of prescription drugs in late 2014, which increased from approximately 7.5% to 16% of all illicit drugs traded through cryptomarkets in a period of less than three months (Soska & Christin, 2015). More detailed subsequent analysis revealed that the increased proportion of prescription drugs sold via cryptomarkets was due almost entirely to a rise in the trading of opioid drugs in the US. Martin et al. (2018a) show that the underlying cause of this large, sustained increase in the trading of illicit opioids was most likely due to new restrictions to the legal scheduling of popularly prescribed opioids by US authorities. This research not only highlights the association with general drug demand and cryptomarket supply, and the embeddedness of cryptomarkets within broader drug markets, but also demonstrates how policy changes – in this case restricting the legal supply of opioid painkillers without implementing demand reduction measures – led to the expansion of the black market for similar drugs.

2.2.2. Non-drug Products

In addition to illicit drugs, cryptomarkets also facilitate a relatively small trade in a variety of other digital and non-digital products. Amongst non-drug products, Kruithof et al. (2016) show that financial products and services, which include money laundering services and stolen/hacked financial accounts and credit card information, are the most popularly traded, followed by physical counterfeit identity documents and associated digital scans, various guides and 'how to' manuals which explain how to commit a variety of illegal activities, as well as equipment used for the commission of non-drug related crime, particularly identity theft (Kruithof et al., 2016). Other products for which markets exist on cryptomarkets but are so small as to be considered negligible include tobacco (Barrera, Malm, Décary-Hétu, & Munksgaard, 2019), exotic wildlife and endangered species (Harrison, Roberts, & Hernandez-Castro, 2016; Wright, 2019).

The relative popularity – or lack thereof – of non-drug goods and services traded on cryptomarkets may be explained by a variety of different factors, some of which are directly or indirectly related to the illicit drugs trade. For example, the trade in stolen credit card information, which enables a variety of fraudulent activities known collectively as 'carding', has a relatively long and independent history on the dark web, with exclusively carding-focused trading forums in operation since the early 2000 (Décary-Hétu & Leppänen, 2013; Holt, Smirnova, & Chua, 2016; Hutchings & Holt, 2017). In much the same way as they facilitate the trading of illicit drugs, cryptomarkets are a natural home to the illegal carding trade given their capacity to facilitate secure and anonymous transactions, their hosting of discussion forums whereby 'carders' can discuss techniques, tips and security measures, and their provision of escrow and customer feedback services which help ensure honesty during transactions.

2.2.3. Weapons

Of the various non-drug products traded on cryptomarkets, weapons are perhaps the least understood by, and the greatest sources of alarm to, the general public and law enforcement agencies. Contrary to sensationalist stories that presented in the news media, the cryptomarket weapons trade is small, with one recent study finding just 23 vendors offering 386 products, including 'non-lethal' weapons such as Tasers, batons and pepper sprays – 25% of the weapons listed were firearms and approximately 5% were explosives (Rhumorbarbe et al., 2018). Importantly, the study also found very limited numbers of recorded customer feedback indicating that 'the number of sales is very low' for this particularly dangerous category of products (Rhumorbarbe et al., 2018, p. 18). The low number of recorded feedbacks does not simply indicate low product turnover, however; it also makes precise quantification of the extent and composition of the cryptomarket weapon trade difficult. This is because fraudulent cryptomarket vendors seeking to scam customers often post fake reviews in order to appear trustworthy (Krylova, 2019; Martin, 2014a; Moeller et al., 2017). Furthermore, law enforcement agencies have been shown to use fraudulent 'honeypot' vendor accounts in order to identify those seeking to purchase weapons on cryptomarkets (Brewster, 2017). These practices render both the limited number of vendors, weapons listings, and what little customer feedback there is highly suspect in comparison to the much larger trade in illicit drugs, and has led one cybersecurity expert to conclude that the majority of cryptomarket weapons sales 'are scams or honeypots set up to ensnare buyers' (Wilson, cited in Brewster, 2017).

The absence of high volume – and therefore more reliable, customer feedback (Martin, 2014a) – poses problems not only for researchers relying on the validity of digital trace data (see Section 3.3.4 for further discussion of the methodological complexities of crawler/feedback data), but also for consumers who, in the absence of voluminous feedback, are diminished in their ability to determine whether or not a weapons vendor is trustworthy (Hardy & Norgaard, 2015). This likely has a significant deterrent effect on purchasing, creating a vicious cycle whereby low sales turnovers create suspicion amongst prospective customers, thereby contributing to fewer future sales and lower associated instances of customer feedback. An additional problem that limits the sale of weapons on cryptomarkets is the relative difficulty of concealing them so as they can be successfully delivered through traditional postal systems. Unlike illicit drugs, which are lightweight and relatively easy to conceal in the post, or digital goods which require no postal delivery at all, weapons in general, and firearms in particular, are bulky, heavy, and typically have metal components, which make them susceptible to interdiction at mail scanning centres, and therefore pose an increased risk of arrest for vendors and consumers alike (Paoli, 2018; Rhumorbarbe et al., 2018). Finally, unlike illicit drugs, for which demand is huge worldwide, demand for weapons appears comparatively low, with the exception of markets such as that in the US.

Despite the limited numbers of weapons traded via cryptomarkets, the effect of firearms sales in particular have been consequential, with at least one case confirmed of a 'lone wolf' terror attack committed in Germany that was perpetrated with a firearm obtained via a cryptomarket (Malik, 2019). This event is likely to have produced a further chilling effect on the already small number of cryptomarket weapons sales due to increased attention from national and transnational law enforcement agencies (see, e.g., EUROPOL, 2016, 2019). Increased attention from law enforcement acts as a deterrent for prospective weapons traders as policing agencies having a strong incentive to create fraudulent buyer accounts in order to conduct undercover buy-bust operations and remove particularly dangerous weapons such as illegal firearms from the black market. This stands in contrast to illicit drugs which, if not available via a cryptomarket are, to a greater or lesser extent, usually still accessible via other means. In other words, being one of the relatively few genuine weapons traders who uses cryptomarkets is a much riskier endeavour than for those who trade in illicit drugs.

When considering the various problems facing both buyers and vendors seeking to use cryptomarkets to trade weapons – scams, honeypots, product uncertainty, difficulties in postal delivery, etc. – it appears that this particular vector of illegal weapons distribution is unusually problematic, suspect and, as a result, limited in its extent, particularly when considered alongside more conventional methods of illegal arms distribution (Dhanapala, Donowaki, & Lumpe, 2019). The lack of popularity of weapons sales amongst buyers and vendors also makes this particular category of products unpopular with cryptomarket administrators. This is because low numbers of weapons sales produce a correspondingly limited number of sales commissions upon which administrator profits are dependent. *Dread Pirate Roberts*, the administrator of

Silk Road 1.0 as well as weapons-only cryptomarket *The Armory*, explicitly cited a lack of turnover as the key factor in his decision to close the site:

> *As most of you have figured out, we are closing the armory. Your first question is probably 'why?'. Well, it just wasn't getting used enough .... The volume hasn't even been enough to cover server costs and is actually waning at this point.*
>
> *(Roberts, 2012)*

When considered in combination, the high risks associated with trading in products that constitute potential threats to national security, and the relatively low amounts of revenues that are generated, are likely responsible for the weapons bans implemented by other market administrators across a minority of cryptomarkets (Paoli, 2018). Given the strong disincentives for market administrators, vendors and consumers seeking to trade weapons via cryptomarkets, and the general unsuitability for the cryptomarket trade in weapons, it appears unlikely that trading activity regarding these products will increase any time soon.

2.2.4. Prohibited Goods and Services

Cryptomarkets are regularly presented in the news media as lawless spaces where practically anything may be bought and sold with impunity (Bond, 2017; Cuthbertson, 2018; Frost, 2019). However, while they lie outside of the realm of state regulation, the notion that *anything* is able to be traded on cryptomarkets is a myth. As alluded to in the previous section, from *Silk Road* on cryptomarket administrators have, for a variety of reasons, continually and voluntarily imposed prohibitions on a range of goods and services. For example, all cryptomarkets observed by the authors have imposed explicit market prohibitions on contract killing and child exploitation material. Similarly, while not necessarily overtly banned on all cryptomarkets, no instances of human trafficking, or the illegal trades in snuff movies or human organs have ever been substantiated.

By trading in some dangerous and illegal goods and services, particularly drugs and weapons, cryptomarket administrators and users obviously bear some responsibility for their public notoriety and nefarious reputation. An additional contributing factor to the widespread public misperception of cryptomarkets, however, is sensationalist and inaccurate newspaper reporting (and, occasionally, poorly conducted academic research) which conflates cryptomarkets with other sites on the dark web, many of which are of dubious credibility. Hitmen services, to take one notable example, have indeed been offered for sale on the dark web, though every case recorded thus far has turned out to be either a scam or a law enforcement honeypot (see Ormsby, 2016, 2018). Similarly, the existence of 'red rooms' which are purported to livestream torture and murders have never been verified by any credible source, though similar sites have been identified on the clear web (AFP, 2017; Ormsby, 2015). By contrast, there is a real and thriving trade in child exploitation material on the dark web (Fonhof, van der Bruggen, & Takes, 2018), though these sharing forums are typically content-specific and are segregated from mainstream cryptomarkets and other dark web sites in a manner analogous to convicted paedophiles being segregated from mainstream prison populations.

As detailed in Chapter 1, since their inception cryptomarkets have, to varying extents, been infused with a radical libertarian political philosophy that rejects unnecessary state-based prohibitions on goods and services in favour of the primacy of the free market (Maddox et al., 2016; Martin, 2014a;

Munksgaard & Demant, 2016; Zajácz, 2017; Zaunseder & Bancroft, 2019). Consistent with libertarian philosophy, however, goods and services may be prohibited if they inevitably involve harm towards others. For some goods and services, questions of harm are contestable, such as the case with firearms which, as in the legal sphere in the US, may be justified on the basis of self-defence. Other products, such as child exploitation material or biological weapons, are unambiguously harmful towards others and are therefore prohibited across all mainstream cryptomarkets. In addition to considerations of harm and the broader social norms prevalent across cryptomarkets, administrators may also ban products that are likely to result in unacceptably high attention from law enforcement or national security agencies. As discussed in the previous section on weapons, these considerations are mediated to some extent by the profitability associated with real or potential trading; from a purely economic perspective, the more profitable a particular good or service, the more likely it is that market administrators will overcome their reservations and permit its trade. The process by which market administrators evaluate these considerations is, of course, subjective, and while there exists a range of common product bans across cryptomarkets as a whole, individual sites differ in the extent to which 'borderline' contentious goods and services are prohibited (e.g. weapons, stolen credit card information).

The peculiar dynamics and nuances associated with cryptomarket prohibitions are perhaps most clearly exemplified by changing attitudes to the synthetic opioid, fentanyl. Prior to the US opioid epidemic, fentanyl was largely unknown outside the medical fraternity, where it remains in common usage as an anaesthetic. As the epidemic spread, however, and access to legal opioids was finally restricted, the black market trade in illicit opioids boomed, overdose deaths increased dramatically, and fentanyl became increasingly recognised as a serious threat to public health (Rudd, 2016). Fentanyl is extraordinarily potent – approximately 40 times stronger than heroin – which makes it not only highly dangerous to consume, but also increases its appeal to drug producers and distributors seeking to increase the potency of their products (Ciccarone, 2017). In recent years, heroin laced with fentanyl has emerged as one of the chief culprits responsible for the staggering increase in opioid-related overdose deaths across much of the US, with the number of fatal overdoses involving opioids adulterated with fentanyl doubling in just two years from 2012 to 2014 (Warner et al., 2016).

Given the widespread demand for opioids and the lack of government initiatives in offering effective demand reduction in the US in particular, it is unsurprising that fentanyl increasingly came to be sold on cryptomarkets, with Martin et al. (2018a) noting a doubling in the proportion of sales of the drug by US vendors between 2014 and 2016. Increasing public alarm about fentanyl and its distribution via cryptomarkets has been further triggered by a variety of media reports, including a 2017 front page expose in the *New York Times* which named the (then) largest cryptomarket in operation, *Alphabay*, as a critical source of distribution (Popper, 2017a). Following the shutdown of *Alphabay* by US authorities later that year, the US Department of Justice (DOJ) overtly highlighted its role as a 'major source of fentanyl' linked to 'multiple overdose deaths across the country' (DOJ, 2017). Then, in 2018, the DOJ, FBI and Drug Enforcement Agency (DEA) and other US agencies executed 'Operation Darkness Falls' specifically targeting cryptomarket sources of fentanyl supply, leading to the arrest of several high-profile fentanyl vendors, and placing further pressure on those who facilitate its sale on cryptomarkets (DOJ, 2018).

These two factors – a growing awareness and hardening of public attitudes towards fentanyl, and increased efforts on the part of law enforcement in cracking down on sources of the drug – provide the social context in which at least three cryptomarkets – *Dream Market*, *Hansa Market* and *Darknet Heroes League* – voluntarily banned the sale of the fentanyl (Popper, 2017b). These bans were accompanied by spirited discussion on cryptomarket forums regarding the appropriate course to take and whether fentanyl was so dangerous so as to warrant some users' classification of it as a 'biological weapon'. Positions were polarised between community members who remained steadfast in their commitment to free-market opposition to any 'top down' restrictions on the sale of fentanyl, and those who advocated prohibiting sales of the drug due to its uniquely deleterious public health effects, and the associated unwelcome attention sales of the drug were drawing from law enforcement agencies (Popper, 2017b). Whether the bans implemented by administrators on the aforementioned cryptomarkets were the result of genuine concern about the dangers of fentanyl or were prompted by a more cynical regard for self-preservation will likely never be known, though these factors are not mutually exclusive.

2.3. IMPACT ON CONVENTIONAL DRUG DISTRIBUTION NETWORKS

The regional clustering that is now apparent for the majority of cryptomarket drug trading carries important implications for our understanding of both the global illicit drugs trade as a whole, as well as for transnational drug distribution networks. Instead of reconfiguring major global drug distribution networks which carry drugs from source countries to the wider world, it appears that cryptomarkets are instead predominantly impacting retail level distribution in consumption countries (Dittus et al., 2017). That is, despite the advent of cryptomarkets and their *potential* to facilitate direct connections between drug suppliers in source countries and customers in consumption countries, conventional transnational drug trafficking networks look to be operating largely as usual, smuggling drugs into consumption countries via conventional means (shipping, air cargo, etc.), and some product is diverged into the cryptomarket supply chain and then posted for local or intraregional sale along the way.

One notable exception in this regard is the Netherlands and its role in the distribution of MDMA. For decades, the Netherlands has been one of the central global production and distribution sources for MDMA (EMCDDA, 2016). However, unlike traditional source countries for other drugs such as cocaine and heroin, the Netherlands has also emerged as the greatest single source of MDMA trafficked internationally via cryptomarkets, accounting for approximately a quarter of global MDMA transactions and revenues (Demant, Munksgaard, Décary-Hétu, et al., 2018). So, why is the Netherlands exceptional amongst production countries in also playing a major role in the global distribution of MDMA on cryptomarkets?

In many ways, the Netherlands is the exception that proves the rule, and there are several factors that are consistent with previous theorising about the nature of the cryptomarket drugs trade which explain its unique position: unlike traditional source countries for other drugs, the Netherlands has both high levels of internet penetration and adoption of cryptocurrency technology, even by European standards (ITU, 2019); Dutch-speaking citizens have high levels of proficiency in English, which facilitates their participation on the majority of cryptomarkets; and the geographic location of the Netherlands in central Europe, and particularly as a member state of the shared customs Schengen Zone, make it a convenient and low-risk supplier for the rest of the continent.

Lastly, Dutch MDMA also has a reputation for high quality and is extraordinarily cheaply priced by international standards, two factors which make it an attractive source country for customers located outside the region.

2.4. HARM REDUCTION

A significant component of cryptomarket research concerns what may broadly be categorised under the theme of harm reduction. In its broadest sense, harm reduction refers to the impact that cryptomarkets have upon the population-level health and wellbeing of societies around the world (Aldridge et al., 2018). Relevant considerations that factor into this complex question include: how cryptomarkets shape the drug using trajectories of individuals (Barratt, Lenton, et al., 2016); the influence of online peer support networks (Bancroft, 2017); whether drugs sold on cryptomarkets are of a higher quality than those that are available through other means (Caudevilla, Ventura, Fornis, et al., 2016), or whether they contain unadvertised adulterants (Quintana et al., 2016); user safety in the process of drug acquisition (Barratt, Ferris, et al., 2016); and whether cryptomarkets lead to a wider range of drugs diffusing into broader illicit markets (Aldridge & Décary-Hétu, 2016). On a systemic level, there is also the possibility that cryptomarkets are reducing drug harms by limiting opportunities for intra-drug market violence (Martin, 2014b, 2014a; Morselli et al., 2017). From the outset, we should caution that despite the growing numbers of studies examining this topic, empirical support for arguments either in favour of, or contrary to the notion that cryptomarkets are reducing drug-related harms is, for the time being, too limited to be conclusive. That said, there is a tentative, though growing consensus amongst researchers that cryptomarkets may indeed be reducing drug-related harms. Below is a summary of some of the main arguments for and against this proposition.

From a user perspective, there is no doubt that cryptomarkets provide greater access to a wider range of drugs than would otherwise be available. For those who are able to access cryptomarkets, drug supply is likely to be more consistent and varied than relying on any number of local dealers. This begs the immediate question, in a context of increased availability, do people who source drugs from cryptomarkets increase the frequency, intensity and variety of their use? Barratt, Lenton et al. (2016) argue that this is precisely the case, but with some important caveats. For the cryptomarket users interviewed by Barratt, Lenton, et al. (2016), being able to access whatever drugs whenever they wanted, notwithstanding delays in postal delivery, resulted in a temporary 'honeymoon' period characterised by elevated levels of consumption of a wider range of illicit drugs (see also Winstock et al., 2019). Following this period, however, users adjusted to the environment of increased abundance and began to adapt their attitudes to drug purchasing and consumption in ways that allowed them to moderate their drug use. This included abandoning previous 'hoarding' behaviours whereby limited access to drugs resulted in purchasing larger quantities than were desired, in favour of only ordering drugs in quantities which were considered appropriate for immediate use. These findings suggest that while drug use and associated harms may intensify in the period immediately following first access to cryptomarkets, these are likely to subside and stabilise shortly thereafter to levels consistent with pre-cryptomarket use.

A key further issue relevant to drug harm concerns whether cryptomarkets are facilitating access to illicit drugs amongst populations who previously did not engage in their use. There is some evidence demonstrating the existence of a relatively small population who, prior to the advent of cryptomarkets, were interested in taking drugs but abstained, either because they lacked access to suppliers or were deterred by the potential dangers or 'shadiness' of undertaking drugs deals 'in real life' (Barratt, Lenton, et al., 2016). For these users, accessing a cryptomarket marked the commencement of their (illicit) drug taking careers. While increases in the overall numbers of people who use drugs are likely to increase both individual and population levels of harm, care needs to be taken in interpreting the relative size and significance of this population. Data from the last five years of the GDS suggests that the vast majority of drug users who access their supply via cryptomarkets already consume illicit drugs, with only 5% of respondents indicating their first ever use following access to a cryptomarket (Winstock et al., 2019). These figures suggest that the growth in the size of the drug using-population resulting from the advent of cryptomarkets is small in relative terms and therefore unlikely to substantially increase attendant harms.

Levels of drug harm are mediated not only by numbers of drug users, but also by the relative quality – or lack thereof – of the drugs which they are consuming. Since 2013, researchers have hypothesised that drugs purchased via cryptomarkets are likely to be of higher quality than those available on 'the street' (Martin, 2014b; Van Hout & Bingham, 2013a). This notion has gained support in recent years, both in terms of user perceptions which suggest that a principle attraction of cryptomarkets is that they offer higher quality products (Masson & Bancroft, 2018; Van Buskirk, Roxburgh, et al., 2016; Van Hout & Bingham, 2014), as well as more objective evidence in the form of forensic sampling which also indicates the presence of fewer adulterants in cryptomarket-purchased drugs (Caudevilla, Ventura, Fornis, et al., 2016). While fewer adulterants may be considered desirable by users, and may also be less dangerous than drugs that are 'cut' with noxious substances, one must also acknowledge the possibility that greater potency/purity may result in greater levels of harm due to the potential effects of drug toxicity and overdose (Scott et al., 2015). A key mediating factor is therefore not only drug purity, but also whether cryptomarket users have adequate knowledge of the composition and potency of the drugs they are taking so as to successfully manage the risks associated with consumption.

Cryptomarket discussion forums offer customers a useful avenue whereby concerns and questions about harm reduction can be discussed amongst a community of interested, though not necessarily well informed, fellow drug users (Bancroft, 2017; Bancroft & Reid, 2016; Masson & Bancroft, 2018; Van Hout & Bingham, 2014). Forums appear to influence harm reduction in several ways, including (1) by offering customers a shared space in which the quality of drugs sold by different vendors may be critiqued, thereby acting as a source of validation to customer feedback provided on seller pages (Masson & Bancroft, 2018); (2) allowing users to share insights into the perceived quality of specific drugs, including whether they have been adulterated, whether they are useful in achieving particular 'highs', and how potent they may be (Bancroft & Reid, 2016); and (3) by facilitating discussion of safer usage practices and appropriate dosing (Van Hout & Bingham, 2014). While some users may be enthusiastic about the role of discussion forums in facilitating information exchange about different forms of harm reduction, it is important to be mindful that the bulk of discussion on these platforms relies upon subjective opinions and folk knowledge of drugs rather than scientifically informed, medically accurate data (Bancroft & Reid, 2016). This leaves forum participants, at best, in a state of reassuring but incomplete knowledge regarding the potential health implications of their drug use.

A further factor influencing drug harms at the macro-level concerns the impact cryptomarkets may be having on broader illicit drug markets. As has been discussed previously in this chapter, cryptomarkets primarily facilitate retail-level drug transactions, with a majority of purchases made for small volumes of drugs considered most likely for personal use (Aldridge & Décary-Hétu, 2016; Christin, 2013). However, this leaves a significant minority of larger-scale transactions (<US$1,000) which are almost certainly intended for further sale and distribution into offline drug markets. Given the wide variety of drugs available on cryptomarkets, this raises the possibility that people who source drugs on cryptomarkets and then sell them offline – so-called business-to-business transactions (Martin, 2014a) – may be diffusing a greater range of illicit drugs into offline drug markets. Aldridge and Décary-Hétu (2016) analyse different categories of drug types sold on cryptomarkets and assess which of these have the highest proportion of wholesale level sales. They conclude that those drug types most likely to be sold for wholesale purposes on cryptomarkets are, in order, MDMA and ecstasy-type drugs, phenethylamines (such as NBOMe, 2-c and 3-c compounds), benzodiazepines, and herbal cannabis. Given that at least two of these drug types – phenethylamines and benzodiazepines – rank highly in terms of relative drug harms and pose significant risks of both fatal and non-fatal toxicity (Kueppers & Cooke, 2015; Nutt, Saulsbury, & Blakemore, 2007), concerns about cryptomarket-facilitated drug diffusion potentially increasing drug harms appear credible.

The harms discussed above concern the effects of illicit drug consumption on user health. However, a further major aspect of drug-related harm results from systemic drug violence which is inadvertently caused by prohibition and the creation of massive black markets that lie outside of state regulation and control. Systemic drug violence is a consequence of physical conflict between drug producers, traffickers, retailers and other offenders, as well as violence between users and those involved in drug distribution. By removing physical interactions between drug traders, and by offering anonymity to retailers, cryptomarkets offer the prospect of reducing systemic drug violence, both for drug users as well as for those who sell drugs online (Martin, 2014a, 2014b; Morselli et al., 2017; Tzanetakis et al., 2016). Tzanetakis et al. (2016) provide some compelling empirical support for this argument in their comparison of threats and actualised violence experienced by suppliers using cryptomarkets and those participating in conventional forms of drug distribution, with the latter proving significantly, and unsurprisingly, more susceptible to systemic violence. In their study of user experiences of violence, Barratt, Ferris, et al. (2016) also conclude that drug consumers are significantly less exposed to systemic violence when sourcing drugs via a cryptomarket, even when compared to closed drug markets in which violence is relatively rare.

The standard justification for drug prohibition is that limiting supply will limit drug use, which will subsequently limit the harmfulness of drugs, both at an individual and societal level. However, the logic underpinning this perspective is dubious, not well supported by empirical evidence and is increasingly being questioned by researchers, policy-makers, medical practitioners and the general public alike (Greer & Ritter, 2019; Hurley, 2017, 2018). As this section has sought to outline, cryptomarkets provide us with something of a window into a post-prohibition world – one in which (technologically privileged) drug users are able to access the illicit substances they desire relatively easily and in a context of comparative safety. When they do so, they appear able to mediate their drug use without the heavy-handed intervention of the state (Barratt, Lenton, et al., 2016). For those who use cryptomarkets to sell drugs, they too appear able to ply their trade while sidestepping some of the systemic, prohibition-related dangers that face their offline counterparts (Tzanetakis et al., 2016). While more research is required to validate the claims presented above concerning the relative harmfulness of cryptomarket drug trading, initial forays into this area hold promise.

2.5. CONCLUDING REMARKS

This chapter has provided an overview of the cryptomarket drugs trade, outlining the size and composition of the cryptomarket trade in terms of drugs as well as other illicit goods and services, discussing the cryptomarket lifecycle and leading causes of mortality, and detailing some of the various trends and issues that have emerged in the few short years since these remarkable sites first came online. What we have witnessed in that time is extraordinary: the creation of a new type of online illicit trading platform, at once individually volatile and also sufficiently stable so as to allow the development of new domestic, regional and, to a more limited extent, international trading networks, each of which is embedded within, impacts upon and is reactive to its particular socio-economic context; the development of new classes of online illicit traders – administrators, vendors and customers – which constitute and contribute to the broader cryptomarket community, and to the ongoing development of social and institutional norms, as well as the political and philosophical debates which underpin them. The novelty, dynamism and sheer technological, social, and criminal ingenuity that has characterised the rise of cryptomarkets is no doubt one of the principal reasons why they have increasingly attracted the attentions not only law enforcement and the general public, but also of those of us in academia whose research methods, ethical views and epistemologies are the subject of the following chapter.

NOTES

1. By contrast, estimates for the cryptomarket-facilitated drugs trade are relatively robust, timely, detailed and methodologically, if not technically, straightforward to conduct. It is ironic that we have a much clearer understanding of drug trading on the so-called 'dark web' than we do in comparison to much more prevalent and long-standing forms of in-person forms of drug exchange.

2. Gwern Branwen is an independent researcher and writer, and a well-respected commentator on cryptomarkets and the dark web drugs trade. His work referenced here is not peer-reviewed, though is comprehensive and reproduced by the EMCDDA & Europol (2017).

3. We note that some speculation remains as to whether this was an actual hack or an inside theft.

3

CRYPTOMARKET RESEARCH METHODS, ETHICS AND EPISTEMOLOGIES

3.1. SCOPE OF THE CHAPTER

Whereas the previous chapter focused on what is known about cryptomarkets, this chapter is concerned with how these pieces of knowledge have been arrived at, what the research methods are that have been deployed and the strengths and limitations of the various approaches that have been used. By reviewing the methods that have been successful, and in some cases unsuccessful, and by integrating these methods into knowledge outlined in the previous chapters, this section of the book shall not only give an overview of what should be considered best practice when it comes to researching cryptomarkets, but also highlight areas where there are opportunities and needs for further refinements and development. Reviewing a large amount of work necessitates a broad and relatively shallow treatment of each, but it is hoped that the references that are mentioned below give the interested reader departure points that they can follow up directly for more detailed discussion of some of the key points. To achieve this aim, the chapter splits broadly into two sections after a brief foray into an overview of the market environment: the first part provides an overview of the main methodological approaches that have been used to attempt to understand the cryptomarket phenomena; with the second outlining some of the issues that are inherently tied to the investigations with suggested avenues for further research.

In dealing with the overview of methodologies, the chapter links to the range of works discussed in the previous section and uses these to demonstrate the utility of the approaches thus far applied. This is not, however, a census of all of the work that has been conducted, merely that which to us seems to be most representative of the whole. Of particular importance to this section is an awareness that any one method can only tell part of the story and due to the complexity and hidden nature of much of the activity on these markets, and their constantly changing subtleties, there is a need to use a triangulation of approaches, from the qualitative to the quantitative, the economic to the sociological. Within this review of the current and existing methods, there will be clearly identified limitations where the tools and methods are still in need of development.

The second section of the chapter is wide ranging. It moves from considering some of the current limitations with the methods that have thus far been used and suggests other possible approaches. In the course of this discussion, it suggests avenues for further research, both methodological and those that break out of the mould of attempting to merely understand the function of these online marketplaces, but also to attempt to use the study of them to uncover broader trends in drug purchasing and usage patterns, and associated artefacts. In doing this, it highlights the central role that theoretical debates can and should play in helping to inform the approaches, and the value that this can bring to a study.

This is followed by a discussion around the ethics of cryptomarket research, and how these fold into questions around internet research more generally. Although this section is all too brief to be thorough, it is hoped that it gives pointers and resources where this understanding can be delved into further. The chapter concludes with a call for more research in this area, and hopefully with an ever-increasing array of methods.

3.2. THE CRYPTOMARKET ENVIRONMENT

Essentially, cryptomarkets consists of three sets of agents – the market administration (including the main administrator(s) and any moderators, web designers and programmers they may employ) that create the actual website(s), the vendor and the purchaser. As the environment is reliant on two key pieces of technology – Tor and cryptocurrencies – both of which, to a greater or lesser extent and given suitable operational security, decouple the identity of the user from the usage (as explained in Chapter 1), this leads to novel set of data being available to the researcher being generated by each of the three components in the system. The first, and most obvious, are the markets themselves. Once Tor has been installed, the web address found and the straightforward task of creating an account overcome, these can be observed and the material within the markets can be used as a basis for research. Cryptomarkets are often described as an 'eBay for drugs' (a phrase originally used by Barratt, 2012) and even a cursory glance at their structure feels familiar to those who regularly buy from online locations. As explained in Chapter 1, the format of these markets was to a greater lesser extent 'set' by the manner in which *Silk Road* was organised, and no doubt drawing on inspiration from the clear web e-commerce sites such as eBay. Each cryptomarket therefore, generally, has:

- an initial landing page, with some information about the market, some loose terms and conditions or perhaps simply a display of some of the more popular products (see fig 3.1);
- a list of product categories that group similar products together although the divisions are not universal and are often in a hierarchy – such as cannabis, with further subdivisions for hash, weed, synthetics, etc. or Ecstasy, with the lower level of MDMA, pills, MDA etc.;
- the individual products themselves, which usually have:
  - a (purported) picture of the product;
  - a description of the product that is on sale often with some detail on the level of purity;
  - the price;
  - where the vendor is willing to ship the product; and
  - from where it will originate;
- the product feedback, generated by people (usernames more often than not anonymised) who have purchased the product usually accompanied by a star rating, a short comment and the date upon which it was posted; and
- a vendor page where any individual seller will give some details about themselves; their terms and conditions; their refund policy; their contact details, which may or may not include their PGP details; some detail that markets themselves as trustworthy or the like; or other general information about themselves and/or products. This section will often aggregate all the feedback that each vendor has received.

Different cryptomarkets have slightly different specifications of each of these components – for instance, an unnamed

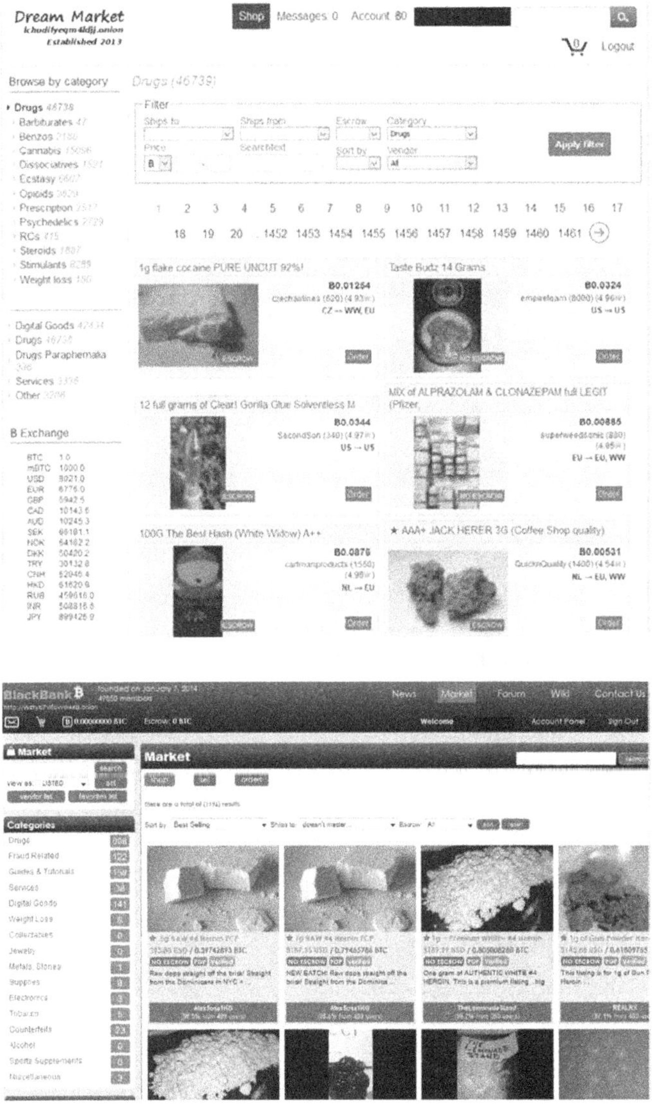

Fig. 3.1. Two Landing Pages, One from *Dream Market* in October 2017 and One from *Black Bank* in May 2015.

market studied by Duxbury and Haynie (2017, 2018) did not anonymise feedbacks, *Dream Market* only displayed the last 40 feedbacks for any product, *Silk Road 3.1* allows orders to be made without creating an account and so on and so forth – small changes but important ones that can sometimes be exploited by the research community.

Each cryptomarket, more often than not, also has a companion forum where vendors can advertise their material, respond to feedback and explain their absences. Similarly, customers can discuss their opinions about the markets, ask general questions, report bugs, request features and post reviews of the various sellers. Cryptomarket administrators also will give announcements, upload guides and tutorials, explain their downtime and generally engage with the community. As with the exact specifics of each market, the level of engagement with any one of the three actors with these forums varies by market and time, nonetheless these are well used and are easily accessed resources.

Beyond forums attached to cryptomarkets, there are a host of related websites that hold discussions about the workings and specifics of the markets. Up until 21 March 2018, Reddit was a primary location for these discussions and specifically the subreddit r/DarkNetMarkets, though with the passing of FOSTA/SESTA laws, Reddit decided to err on side of caution and remove this content from their platform (Cimpanu, 2018; reddit, 2018). New forums opened in various locations on both the clear and the dark web, with the most prominent being known as *Dread* which has deliberately styled itself as a Reddit replacement. Finally, there are websites dedicated to covering cryptomarket activity that fulfil journalistic/informative roles. DeepDotWeb was very much on the journalistic side and held up to date listings of markets, with some measure of their active 'up time' (the percentage of time that the markets are available), reports of news related to cryptomarkets and the wider drug trade, and often interviews with market administrators during the launch of a new market or the like (as explained in section 1.5.3 DeepDotWeb was closed in May 2019)

Overall, although there are similarities between cryptomarkets, the discussion forums and the wider places on the internet where the community meets, and the attached journalistic/harm reduction websites, these are all in constant flux. Keeping up with the developments in the community relies on key node websites which themselves may disappear at any moment. Researching these communities and websites therefore requires the observer to submerse themselves in the field, to read widely and engage with a variety of sources and actors to be able to understand the workings of the wider environment. Beyond reading, one must have a basic understanding of Tor, of PGP, of the dark web structure, of .onion addresses and Bitcoin, encryption and operational security. One must lurk in forums such as *Dread* or those attached to cryptomarkets, make accounts with the various markets themselves and explore their organisation; one must become familiar with the journalistic websites and the works of some of the journalists who report on the activity within the space. To paraphrase Robert Park, one must get one's digital trousers dirty in real world research. In much the same way that Kowalski et al. (2019) describe learning to purchase from cryptomarkets, there is a period of liminality and self-reliance that the researcher must go through to be able to successfully uncover the nature of these markets.

3.3. METHODS AND APPROACHES USED TO-DATE

As demonstrated in the first two chapters of this book, the developments of both cryptomarkets and cryptomarket research have been fast paced. Since the initial launch of *Silk*

Road in February 2011, it was only four months before it was brought to the wider attention of the world through a Gawker article (Chen, 2011) and the research community was quick to react. Barratt (2012) penned a short notification in February imploring the research community to 'definitely watch this space' (p. 107), and this was quickly followed by four pieces of work that set the scene for much of the research methodologies that followed: qualitative approaches (Van Hout & Bingham, 2013a, 2013b); survey research (Barratt, Ferris, & Winstock, 2014); and what has become to be known as the 'digital trace' method as a form of webometrics (Christin, 2013). Since these initial works, there have been 120 publications as listed on Web of Science and Scopus[1] with a steadily increasing number of citations published by 230 different authors (see fig 3.2). These worked have appeared in drug policy journals, criminology, psychiatry, computer science, pharmacology, medical, legal and other publications which do not fall into neat classifications.

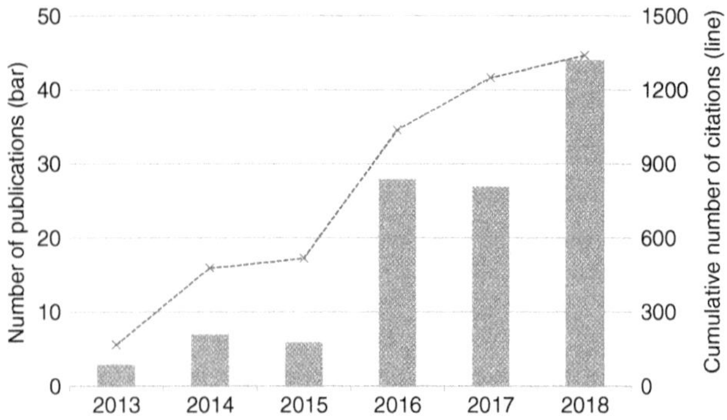

Fig. 3.2. Number of Publications and Cumulative Number of Citations from Web of Science/Scopus, 2013 to 2018 (as at 25 March 2019).

3.3.1. Qualitative Approaches

As is often the case in an arena where there is little pre-existing knowledge, qualitative approaches can provide an insight into what is occurring and help develop knowledge. Van Hout and Bingham's (2013a) first foray into this domain was a single case study of a *Silk Road* user's 'motives for online drug purchasing, experiences of accessing and using the website, drug information sourcing, decision making and purchasing, outcomes and settings for use, and perspectives around security' (Van Hout & Bingham, 2013a, p. 385) with the user initially recruited through an extended conversation on the *Silk Road* chat forum. Their second piece, submitted eight months after their initial work, followed a similar methodology, although this time made use of the chat forum observation data directly and combined this with 20 anonymous online interviews. The final part of this three-phase project again took a similar approach and used the rapport in the discussion forums garnered by Bingham to interview, via encrypted chat channels, 10 vendors over a six-month period. These three exploratory pieces investigated motives for, and processes of, use of cryptomarkets, the market dynamics of the early *Silk Road* and the fears that the community felt about the possible longevity of the ecosystem at the time.

Similar interview style investigations have been carried out by a range of different investigators, with both buyers and vendors. Barratt, Lenton, et al. (2016) interviewed 17 *Silk Road* drug purchasers about their experiences of cryptomarkets between 2012 and 2014 from a harm reduction perspective, finding a complex picture with some users experienced an increase in usage upon first discovering cryptomarkets, but over a longer term reduced hoarding and a feeling they were able to manage their drug use with less worry about supply. Maddox et al. (2016) drew on the same set of interviews, and discussed how technological developments and solutions within the cryptomarket scene could be used to build a more permissive digital reality for those stigmatised through their illicit drug use, which they refer to as constructive activism.

Alongside the direct qualitative interviewing of various types of people who are involved with the cryptomarket drug trade, the related forums and discussion threads where people share information have also been used and analysed qualitatively. For instance, Ladegaard (2017a) investigation of social cohesion on cryptomarkets drew on discussion data on both *Silk Road* and *Silk Road 2* forums in the six months after the seizure of *Silk Road*, and analysed how the community had responded to the disruption with solidarity and reinforcement of their moral positionality to move to other websites; Morselli et al. (2017) revisit questions of conflict that Tzanetakis et al. (2016) first touched on and examine social controls and conflict management via inspection of the terms and conditions of the 10 most popular markets alongside analysis of 200 discussion threads between buyer, vendor and market administrator on the 'official forum of one of the largest cryptomarkets at the time of writing' (Morselli et al., 2017, p. 243). Van Hout and Hearne (2017) is another work to take a harm reduction perspective, this time focussing on NPS, monitor discussion threads relating to NPS and apply a 'phenomenological psychological five step method' (Van Hout & Hearne, 2017, p. 104) to build a set of themes and categories of discussion. They conclude that monitoring such spaces can lead to knowledge about emerging drug trends – and highlight benzodiazepines as an emerging problem product group (an issue later confirmed by Cunliffe et al., 2019).

Using both qualitative interview and analysis of forum data has been shown to be able to be combined to cover more ground. Bancroft and Reid (2016) take a harm reduction perspective and utilised such a two-stage method that incorporated both analysis of forum data and qualitative interviews with users, to study perceptions of drug quality on cryptomarkets. Their investigation found that 'quality' meant more than just the chemical makeup of the products being bought and captured ideas of reliability, purity, potency and predictability which was judged across a number dimensions ('embodied, craft and chemical' – p. 42). Masson and Bancroft (2018) drew on interviews with nine users of drug cryptomarkets along with overt non-participant observation of a cryptomarket forum and found that the marketplaces function as more than just 'perfect markets' and that there is a semblance of community, though a community that is not immune to risk of scams, hacks and threats. Their usage of both interviews and observation of the wider community allowed a 'thick' descriptive analysis of how morality of exchange is controlled on cryptomarkets and find that internet activity is different but similarly seen as 'real' as the parallel offline world (in their words – 'meatspace'). Kowalski et al. (2019) investigate the question of why cryptomarkets are not more widely used, focussing on perceived ease of use, and draw on data from seven face to face interviews with users of cryptomarket alongside 350 hours of structured observations of forums.

3.3.2. Survey Data

Survey data on the usage of cryptomarkets are relatively rare: questions about these relatively new phenomena have not yet permeated onto the usual large-scale data collections exercises conducted by national governments or large-scale research agencies and resultant dataset such as the Crime Survey for England and Wales, the Australian National Drug Strategy Household Survey, the US National Survey on Drug Use and Health, the

Epidemiological Survey of Substance Abuse (ESA) or Drug Affinity Study (DAS) in Germany. To date, any survey data on usage rates, the factors associated with cryptomarket use or any other artefacts suitable for survey data collection have come from data collection exercises that have been developed by specialised teams that have a specific interest in cryptomarkets.

Primary amongst these is the GDS, which first included a question about cryptomarkets in late 2012 (the question: 'Have you ever bought drugs from *Silk Road*?' came with the answer categories: never heard of Silk Road; Have heard of, but never bought; and have consumed drugs purchased from *Silk Road*) which was used as the basis for the first paper that looked at the prevalence of awareness of *Silk Road* (Barratt et al., 2014). Out of the 9,470 respondents in the sample Barratt et al. (2014) analyse

> *a total of 65% of US, 53% of Australian and 40% of UK respondents had heard of SR; 18% of US, 10% of UK and 7% of Australian respondents had consumed drugs purchased through SR.*

As will be discussed later in this section, the work stays away from making claims about whether this awareness prevalence represents anything about overall awareness, but investigate the reasons why people used, or don't use, *Silk Road* – with answer generally related to ease of access, safety and prices, but varying by location. Since then, the question set used to ask about cryptomarket usage and awareness have expanded within each wave of the GDS, with the 2018 questionnaire asking a range of questions about purchasing habits for different drugs types, perceptions of purity, availability, quality, usage of forums for information and perceptions of how the markets themselves have developed over time.

Due the nature of the data collection process and the manner in which the GDS frames itself, however, there are some significant limitations as to the availability and usage of this resource. The GDS is self-funded, having grown from a survey first developed to study the drug use and the nightlife economy on behalf of *Mixmag*, a UK based electronic dance and clubbing magazine. While it now partners with a number of different organisations, this independent ethos remains the same and the data collection is proudly not beholden to any funding body. To that end, the business model is 'the reverse' of the usual academic model – data is collected from its existing money and the resultant data is made available for researchers to purchase access to after it is collected (Barratt et al., 2017). This certainly brings a range of benefits – not least the very fact that the team are able to react to new and developing drug trends and included detailed questioning about them without being beholden to external parties that may slow down the process, as the very inclusion of questions about cryptomarkets back in 2012 demonstrates – just a year and half after *Silk Road* had launched.

The GDS adopts a non-probability sampling strategy of those who have used drugs, essentially anyone who decides to answer it, with the stated aim of capturing information from the participants who are viewed as the experts on drug use. The survey therefore suffers from the usual and well known issues of representativeness and generalisability common to all non-probability sampling methods (see Schonlau & Couper, 2017). Barratt et al. (2017), in a paper entitled *Moving On from Representativeness: Testing the Utility of the Global Drug Survey*, find that the age and sex distribution of those who had recently used cannabis did not differ substantially between the non-probability sampling of the GDS and probability sample in the US, Australia and Switzerland even if the reported usage rates were higher in the GDS than any of the three comparator surveys. The authors are clear, the GDS is not, and never will be, suitable to answer questions about overall population level usage rates of cryptomarkets or any other questions about drug usage prevalence, but they balance the aims of the data collection of the GDS, with its focus on gathering information from a hard to reach population, against the need for representativeness and report that the use of opt-in web surveys are an efficient way to gain a deep understanding of possibly stigmatising behaviours as long as the source is not used to estimate drug use prevalence at a population level. The clear issue, therefore, does not lie in the publications that are produced by GDS researchers, but with how these numbers are subsequently understood by users of the findings who are perhaps not fully aware of these nuances – a warning that should be applied to the findings reported in Section 2.1.1.

Other survey data collection appears hard to come by – the only example of which we know was conducted by Van Buskirk, Roxburgh, et al. (2016) who recruited a sample of 800 regular psychostimulant users in Australia and subsequently asked them about their usage of cryptomarkets in the previous year, their demographics, drug use, criminal activity and mental health. Again, due to the nature of their sampling frame, they do not make claims about overall population levels, but do report on the characteristics of cryptomarket users (younger, more likely to be involved in property crime, heavier/more varied drug usage) though the work suffers from having only 68 respondents (9% of the sample) who had used cryptomarkets to buy drugs.

3.3.3. Digital Trace, from the Markets

Of the 125 papers that have been published and used in Fig. 3.2, over 40% have drawn on what has come be known as 'digital trace' methods (Décary-Hétu & Aldridge, 2015), named after the phrase first used by Venturini and Latour (2009) in a much wider context encapsulating the opportunities that digital information presents to social scientists in general. In this broad context, the phrase digital trace refers to the broad spectrum of information that is recorded in a digital context by the actions of individuals or organisations in an online environment. Initial proponents of the utility of digital trace felt that this would usher in a new phase in the social sciences where theory could be replaced by atheoretical big data – a dream that has perhaps not yet been realised (Hepp, Breiter, & Friemel, 2018). In the context used here, it is much narrower, and relates purely to that which Décary-Hétu and Aldridge (2015) define as the traces (or records) left on the markets (and forums, in Section 3.3.5) themselves.

First used to study cryptomarkets by Christin (2013), this method involves downloading then storing (i.e. a process of crawling the websites) followed by processing and organising (i.e. scraping) the actual webpages present on the markets and using these as the basis for research. The crawling stage can be carried out by custom software (Aldridge & Décary-Hétu, 2014; Soska & Christin, 2015) or some pre-packaged solution such as HTTrack (Christin, 2013; Dolliver, 2015) and there are numerous variations on the exact approach that can be used, but all require some level of technical skill to be able to set up the systematic downloading procedures and the parsing of the resultant information to make it into an analysable form. Data have been collected from single markets, multiple markets, at one time point or repeatedly over time.

Varying levels of complexity of data wrangling and analysis have been used, that have drawn on different aspects of the data present on the markets, with some parts of the data that still remain unanalysed. Van Buskirk, Naicker, et al. (2016) manually downloaded every page from the *Agora* marketplace between mid-February and mid-March 2015 and used a visual basic for applications (VBA) parsing process to separate out the listing description, vendor name, country of origin and substance category to study regional differences in listings and number of vendors. A similar team of researchers in Van Buskirk et al. (2017) then investigated how market closures effect vendor numbers across 39 different cryptomarkets between October 2013 and November 2015. This work again used a manual approach to opening each page on each cryptomarket, this time on a weekly basis, with VBA again used to extract date of collection, listing description, vendor name and the name of the cryptomarket from which it was extracted. Ladegaard (2019) collected data between October 2014 and November 2015 using a python script and combined vendor names, prices and market feedback (to proxy transactions) to investigate the effect on the Dutch MDMA market that the arrest of a particularly successful vendor, HollandOnline. Norbutas (2018) used an extract of a publicly available data archive of cryptomarkets covering the period 2013–2015 that was collected by the independent research Gwern Branwen and is available online for download (Branwen et al., 2015). This archive covers crawls from 89 markets with vendor pages, images, feedbacks and listings, more than 37 related forums and was collected on weekly basis from 2013 through to 2015. It consists of HTML files which must be 'scraped', the process in which the data are extracted, before being analysable. Norbutas (2018) focused on the *Abraxas* market, with data from December 2014 to July 2015, and made use of the fact that on this particular market customer names were not anonymised. This information was combined with identification of vendors and used to construct a network to uncover the geographical clustering of purchasing patterns – finding clustering with postal jurisdictions, predominantly within country but particularly within continent. This usage of the quirks of one particular market is a good example of what can be achieved given an awareness of the particular attributes of specific markets. Another example is the use of sellers advertised stock, which Nurmi et al. (2017) collected from the market Silkkitie finding it to be positively associated with a vendor's daily sales.

Branwen's data archive has been used for numerous papers (e.g. Demant et al. 2018; Moeller et al., 2017; Munksgaard, Bakken, S., & Demant, 2017; Norbutas, 2018). Décary-Hétu and Giommoni (2017) use the data to investigate the effect of Operation Onymous (see Chapter 1 for an overview of this law enforcement operation) on the overall size of the markets, and discuss in detail in the completeness of the information present in the publicly available archive, finding if not a complete picture of the markets, then at least a very good approximation and outline the steps they took to adjust for any inaccuracies. The dataset was also used by Munksgaard, Demant, and Branwen (2016) to re-analyse findings first put forward by Dolliver (2015). This original paper had used data collected, presumably by the author but later revealed to be under a non-disclosure agreement, from *Silk Road 2* on 3 September 2014 and was framed as a complete crawl of the market, and was used to investigate the different types and numbers of items for sale on *Silk Road 2*. Munksgaard et al. (2016) contest the finding from the previous paper, finding the *Silk Road 2* marketplace to have been much bigger than the description given by Dolliver and lacking the latter's claim of a significant number of ebooks, despite acknowledging the incompleteness of their own data when contrasted against Dolliver's claims of completeness. Munksgaard et al. (2016) go onto outline four steps that researchers should go through before using a data collection to make firm claims: quality should be assessed through analysis of error logs; downloaded content should be checked for validity; data should be as open access as possible, if not the entire dataset then at least significant components of metadata made available; and scepticism should be the default position, with data critically compared to other sources with an expectation of inaccuracy.

Given the technical complexity of accurately capturing the market environment through scraping methods that rely on the Tor network and are aimed at markets which do not necessarily follow best web design practice, it is perhaps unsurprising that two of the more influential papers have been published by computer scientists. As mentioned Christin (2013) was the first to use webometrics to assess the size of the *Silk Road* trade, with the later paper by Soska and Christin (2015) analysing how overall trade across all markets has changed over time between mid-2013 and mid-2015. At around the same time, Aldridge and Décary-Hétu (2014) published their first paper that drew on their own data collection tool. The pair (Décary-Hétu & Aldridge, 2015) subsequently published a paper that outlined three different ways to study offenders who operate online – mirroring (i.e. scraping), monitoring (observing) and utilising leaks of information. The paper outlines the development of the tool they name DATACRYPTO that has gone on to be used in at least 20 peer reviewed papers (number imprecise due to language barriers) and subject to at least three major grants, and through numerous developments and iterations.

As the most prominent of the data collection tools used to study cryptomarkets, and one that all the authors of this book have a good knowledge (Cunliffe et al., 2019, 2017; Demant, Munksgaard, Décary-Hétu, et al., 2018; Martin et al., 2018b, 2018a) it is possible to generalizing from the DATACRYPTO approach to a sensible and flexible way to extract, process and store cryptomarket data: either during or after crawling a website, products, sellers and feedbacks are parsed and extracted (the scraping process) which is then stored in a base format that consists of three tables (stored as a .csv file, or the like) containing observations of products, sellers and feedback per crawl with associated metadata (e.g. rating, country of origin, price). If the three tables share common identifiers for sellers and products, this allows a high degree of flexibility as the tables are easily combined. For example, the number of vendors trading within a certain drug category per country can be calculated with relative ease by combining product and seller observations. By storing a continuous record, it also becomes possible to construct longitudinal designs; for example, it would be possible to measure how the number of vendors within a specific drug category has changed over time by combining data over multiple crawls.

Using the number of feedback received for each product or seller has become an established proxy for transactions amongst scholars (Aldridge & Décary-Hétu, 2014; Christin, 2013; Décary-Hétu & Aldridge, 2015; Kruithof et al., 2016; Soska & Christin, 2015), though it is acknowledged to underestimate the actual number of transactions with an estimated coverage between 71% and 88% of transactions suggested by Kruithof et al. (2016, pp. 14–15). From the combination of these sources of data at the level of the vendor, products and feedback, scholars can calculate aggregated metrics like active products (i.e. those that have sold within the previous 30 days), country of origin, vendor revenue or construct network measures (Demant, Munksgaard, Décary-Hétu, et al., 2018; Kruithof et al., 2016; Norbutas, 2018; Soska & Christin, 2015).

Scraping the raw HTML (aka parsing) can be time-consuming and the information that can be derived from a crawl is worth separating into what is available as *fields* and *in-text*. Fields are extractable based on the fields present in the coding of the website (such as the price, or the location of shipping origin) using tools like CSS-selectors, XPath- and regular expressions. However, there is little quality control of what the creators of the listing are required to enter into each field – the cost of a poorly set up listing is felt only by the vendor who is less likely to make sales. As such, even the most well-constructed parsing method is likely to result in errors to the classifications of some fields, with data quality for all fields in need of careful and systematic analysis for errors. Unless available as a field, some information is only available *in text*, generally in the product title[2] or description.[3] Such variables may be the quantity, category, drug type or advertised purity. Consequently, scholars must either resort to manual coding or use automated approaches.

Kruithof et al. (2016) report the steps that are used to clean the data and various data quality concerns with DATACRYTPO, listing a set of issues that need to be considered when using the data and outline the methods used to define their dataset. These are: how to treat holding prices; how the number of transactions are counted; how monthly revenues are estimated; how shipping routes are identified; how products are categorised; how product quantities and purities are estimated; how duplicated vendors are identified; and how stealth listings (i.e. those listing which are private) are dealt with. The interested reader is referred directly to that publication for more information on the methods applied and this work will touch on just two of the processes used – how purities/quantities are derived and how shipping routes are defined. It should be clearly noted that these techniques that are described in Kruithof et al. (2016) were not created solely for that one report, and have been applied to numerous works based on DATACRYTPO, and other work that has also taken a digital trace methodology have following similar methods (including those works listed earlier in this section). Much of the processing of the data was conducted manually by a team of researchers. This was particularly applied to the shipping routes, quantities and advertised purities. As much as was possible, this initially relied on the scraped data, after which *human* coders were used – for example, to extract the quantity of product in each listing from the title or reading the shipping routes and making a decision on the most likely source country. An alternate approach to human coding is the use of supervised learning for classification tasks (Soska & Christin, 2015), but good performance will still require training data that is coded manually or is of high quality.

In short, building a dataset capable of addressing a wide range of research questions and constructing an analysable version of as much of the data on markets as possible is time consuming, resource intensive and difficult endeavour. Within the process of the development and analysis of these data there are some informal best practices that have been arrived at, such as how to match unique vendors, how to proxy sales, how to calculate revenues, how to combine drug types and the nuances that any analysis needs to take into account. DATACRYPTO is not alone as a data collection tool, and other researchers have also used this digital trace methodology to great effect (as discussed earlier in this section), but the 'back catalogues' present in these data, in DATACRYPTO and Branwen's scarpes, are a valuable resource that have considerable amounts of data that remain underutilised, particular amongst these are a huge amounts of free text, and this is a point that will be returned to later in this chapter.

3.3.4. Digital Trace, from Elsewhere

Digital trace information has not just been retrieved and analysed directly from the markets but has also drawn on information from the market forums, in an analogous manner to the way qualitative approaches have interviewed market participants and alternatively drawn on forum data. In order to make sense of the large amount of text data that are present in these forums, these papers have often made use of more advanced textual analysis techniques to be able to manage the sheer quantity of data they are face with. For example, Moeller et al. (2017) focus on 'predatory resource exchange similar to robberies and process-based fraudulent resource exchange similar to rip-offs' (Moeller et al., 2017, p. 1427) and use two complementary techniques to understand the dynamics: a combination of 'lurking' (Moeller et al., 2017, p. 1432) and actively monitoring on Reddit forums for 18 months; and supplement this applying unsupervised text classification using correlated topic modelling based on the forum data collected in Branwen's (2015) archive. These supplemental data were used to add empirical evidence to that which they collected through lurking. Branwen's (2015) archive of forum posts was also drawn on by Munksgaard and Demant (2016) who again applied unsupervised topic modelling, with a qualitative check on the results to make sure it had the 'ability to produce coherent topics and capture topics discussed in the literature on cryptomarkets (e.g. harm-reduction, libertarian politics) and obvious topics such as smuggling, dealing, and discussion of substances' (Munksgaard & Demant, 2016, p. 80). Their work found a decline in the prevalence of political debate on the markets over the study frame (2011 to the end of 2013) as detailed in Section 1.4.2.

In a similar unsupervised topic modelling vein, Porter (2018) used Latent Dirichlet Allocation on a dataset retrieved from r/DarkNetMarkets between November 2016 and November 2017, split into monthly chunks, and extracted trends relating to criminal activity and their methods, finding evidence that users of the dark web were becoming increasingly security minded due to recent law enforcement events. The ideas of trust, community and discourse were further explored by Lorenzo-Dus and Cristofaro (2018), and again based on Branwen's (2015) archive – though with a tighter focus on just Silk Road (1) and Silk Road 2 forums, looked at how the two communities constructed ideas of trust. They used a Corpus Assisted Discourse Studies approach and compared occurrences of specific words to a specifically built corpus they name the 'drug policy making' corpus comprising all the reports that were published by the United Nations Office on Drugs and Crime (UNODC) in 2012 and 2013. Their results parallel those of Porter (2018) in finding that law enforcement activity encourages the community to look for technological innovations to protect the markets, even if these innovations were not then, in the main, acted up on (see Section 1.5.1).

3.3.5. Test Buys

A distinct theme of research used to date has been deployed to address the perception that cryptomarket vendors supply 'better quality' products (Aldridge & Décary-Hétu, 2014; Barratt et al., 2014; Martin, 2014a; Van Hout & Bingham, 2014). These have taken the form of test buys followed by chemical testing to ascertain the contents of what was available for sale. Necessarily, these approaches have been limited in scale, having weighed and/or analysed just a handful of purchases. Caudevilla et al. (2016) were the first to publish using this approach, and made use of the Spanish non-governmental organisation Energy Control's International Drug Testing Service, which offered a chromatography testing service for a cost of €50 'advertised only to cryptomarket users' via adverts placed on *Silk Road 2* and *Evolution* forums. The paper reports results from 219 samples received between March 2014 and March 2015 received from Europe (42%), Australia (26%), US (21%), China (5%),

Canada (3%) and surprisingly, given how infrequent it appears on cryptomarkets in general (Martin et al., 2018b), Argentina with 3% – though this was just six samples. The majority of the substances tested were cocaine (103 samples) with some LSD, MDMA (either pill or crystal), amphetamine, ketamine and cannabis. The team tentatively conclude that 'the purity of our sample of cryptomarket-sourced substances appears relatively high in comparison to other published research' (Caudevilla, Ventura, Fornís, et al., 2016, p. 7). The Energy Control testing service has also published on more specific drugs types: Quintana et al. (2016) analysed four samples received by the service and tested for the fentanyl analogue ocfentanil.

Other testing works have used either test buys or made use of national samples available to the researchers. Rhumorbarbe et al. (2016), for example, ordered four products available from Swiss vendors, with one of those being a repeat buy, and report on the shipping, concealment during postage (aka the 'stealth' used by the vendor) and purity of the products purchased. They find that data presented on the markets in these four cases were generally accurate (shipping times, concealment methods) but that purity was different (and worse). Van der Gouwe, Brunt, van Laar, and van der Pol (2017), on the other hand, analysed data from the Dutch Drugs Information and Monitoring System, which offers anonymous drug testing at addiction care centres throughout the Netherlands. They analysed 32,663 samples, 928 were reported as being purchased through online outlets that were submitted between January 2013 and January 2016, with the proportion of online samples increasing over that time frame. Their findings indicate that the purity of cryptomarket produce was marginally better in some drug groupings (4-FA, MDMA powder and ecstasy pills) than that bought through traditional routes.

3.4. METHODOLOGICAL LIMITATIONS AND IMPLICATIONS

3.4.1. Current Limitations and Other Possible Methods

There are some clear areas where more research can be used to deepen our understanding of cryptomarkets – some of which appear relatively simple, some which require technical skills and some of which require a deeper understanding of the dynamics of drug markets, the nature of cryptomarkets, criminological theory, or all of the above.

One area of analysis that has been notable by its low prominence is an analysis of the prices of products sold on cryptomarkets, despite the fact that this information is obviously present in the digital trace data. This is for good reason, namely adjusting for package size/purity and making justifiable 'apples with apples' comparisons to other traditional pricing data – a problem common to at least two other papers than the following discussion (Hardy & Norgaard, 2015; Przepiorka et al., 2017). Cunliffe et al. (2017), for example, while investigating the prices of drugs available to Australian cryptomarket compare the prices of various drugs from either Australian based or international vendors, and then go onto to compare this to street prices. In the comparison between Australian based and international vendors, the work controls for weight, purity, and specific drug type based on the same dataset as used by Kruithof et al. (2016) who had gone to great lengths to clean the data (Section 3.3.4). When it came to comparing online to street prices, there were two barriers. The first was getting reliable street prices, and the paper drew on findings from the Ecstasy and Related Drugs Reporting System (Sindicich, Stafford, & Breen, 2016), the best available source, but one itself based on small samples of interviews with drug purchasers and focusing on specific quantities of various drugs. The second barrier was attempting to find comparable products from online sources to match the offline data collection specifications, and the work drastically trimmed down the sample, from over 50,000 products to just 1,294 spread over 10 categories. In some groupings, results were presented on a sample of just 37 products listed on cryptomarkets – the very border of reliability. Therefore, despite the appearance of a 'big data' approach, when specified appropriately, sample size quickly became an issue.

Controlling for differences in package size and purity is a difficult task as these fields are not automatically separable – a problem common across studies and not limited to just DATACRYPTO work (see Hardy & Norgaard, 2015; Przepiorka et al., 2017). While research teams have made some steps to address this issue it does highlight an area where more developments can be made. Not only is there scope to use automated methods such as supervised text classification methods to extract the data available *in-text*, in the longer product descriptions or vendor self-descriptions. For instance – shipping methods are generally taken as an unavoidable extra expense and no work thus far has looked deeply into how they vary by region, nor has there been any work that has looked specifically and quantitatively at refund polices. These pieces of information are buried in the text that is added by the vendor on either the product or vendor pages, is often highly irregular with numerous special characters, and spread across the markets. Regardless, there remains a lot of information *in-text* which is not easily collected using scraping but must either be coded manually or using tools like supervised classification.

The methodological limitations inherent to digital trace do not stop there, with a further example being when looking at the economic angle of the markets – how much revenue they make. To date this has relied on using feedback to proxy sales, and then using the listing price to estimate revenue. The tacit assumption is that the purchaser buys just one multiple of each product (unless the feedback structure on a specific cryptomarket gives more detail, but this is not always the case). There is, however, nothing stopping someone from buying multiple products from one listing, in much the same way one may buy multiple light bulbs from a site on the clear web. On the majority of the markets that have thus far been in existence, this would be calculated under the current methodologies as one purchase at whatever quantity the listing has in the title, ignoring those buyers who click to buy multiples.[4] By contrasting digital traces retrieved from the markets with digital information from elsewhere, however, this could be solvable. As all transactions use cryptocurrencies to make their payment, and the very essence of the blockchain is a publicly available ledger system that records all payments permanently, then it is possible to analyse the blockchain to calculate the amount of money flowing into and out of cryptomarkets. This relies on the actual markets wallets being identified, but there has been a good deal of work that has attempted to analyse blockchains to understand how, and by who, cryptocurrencies are used (Foley, Karlsen, & Putniņš, 2019; Harlev et al., 2018; Kuzuno & Karam, 2017). Not only would this allow estimates of market revenues it would also illuminate the accuracy of the feedback/sales proxy method.

This type of multiple perspective digital trace analysis quickly runs into: (1) ethical issues, as this type of analysis could be used to de-anonymise participants of the market environment – a discussion that will be returned to in the ethics section below; and (2) analytical issues – finding which wallets correspond to cryptomarkets can be found through some level of test purchases and tracking, but depending on the market infrastructure can be extremely complex. It does however point to a truth. Digital trace methods in the narrow sense as described thus far have almost universally focused on information retrieved from either the markets directly or their related forums. These works have illuminated much about the working of cryptomarkets and some aspects of drug policy beyond that – but is there a risk that researchers are becoming too reliant on them, and that this reliance is hindering more wide-ranging new methodologies? The allure of statistical certainty and the novel attractiveness of 'big data' are certainly draw factors, but researchers should make space to incorporate multiple mixed-methods perspectives. As has been mentioned in passing earlier in this chapter, Van Hout and Hearne (2017) found evidence of increasing levels of benzodiazepines being discussed on forums, and it wasn't until two years later that Cunliffe et al. (2019) revisited this domain and focused on prescription psychiatric drugs, albeit with a slightly different focus, and found quantitative evidence of these increases. Ladegaard (2017c), for instance, presents an excellent example of mixed methods which combines digital trace information and qualitative readings, as will be discussed in section 3.4.2. Developing research strategies that cross methodological divides and triangulate various different approaches is therefore appropriate for studying the complex phenomena of cryptomarkets.

Limitations to research are not limited to the quantitative digital trace approaches, solvable by ever increasing levels of computerised analytical complexity, but are also present in the other domains. The GDS and surveys of drug users more generally are constrained by their hard to reach populations and purposeful non-probability sampling strategies that need to be deployed, and therefore a wide range of possible research questions are outside of their remit. Would the deployment of a similar data-collection strategy as the GDS aimed at generalisability to the population be possible within the confines of a typical social science research budget? The answer, while cryptomarkets occupy a relatively niche way to purchase drugs, is probably a no, but should their popularity continue to grow, as is hypothesised in this book, then perhaps there will come a point where there will be sufficient people to be able to sample from the population and gather enough data on those who have used cryptomarkets to allow more traditional social science analytical techniques to be used.

Qualitative data are limited for an almost entirely different set of reasons. Analysis of forum data from a qualitative perspective is beset by the usual issue of representativeness, and with such a vast amount of material out there upon which to draw, quickly get subsumed by these problems. Not all 'action' takes place within the purview of researchers, such as dispute resolutions and personal messages (Morselli et al., 2017). These may substantively change the context of the interaction between two parties yet remain hidden. Work which has tried to understand the methods of conflict resolution, or of market dynamics, should therefore typically operate under the assumption that some key information is unobservable, both in content and quantity. On a more personal level, in depth interviews – with buyer, vendors or market administrators/moderators – could prove to be hugely illuminating but the main barrier here is access. Will people be willing to participate with 'any-old' researcher, especially given the particularly high level of fear of law enforcement action? Barratt and Maddox (2016) explain the lengths they went to gain trust and access to their populations of *Silk Road* users (Barratt, Lenton, et al., 2016; Maddox et al., 2016) and drew on their considerable standing as active members of a drug-harm reduction website and generally being well known and respected contributors to the academic side of the cryptomarket environment to enable their work to be successful. Building similar levels of trust and gaining access for other researcher projects will be time consuming and require significant effort, and this should not be underestimated.

3.4.2. Importance of Interdisciplinary Work and Theory

The early cryptomarket work bore the hallmarks of simply investigating the phenomena and explaining their existence – even if this was (tacitly) from a certain theoretical angle, such as economic sociology, social control or moral boundary setting (as highlighted earlier). As the field has developed, with tools and methodologies being establishing, more recent work has started to get to grips with what these markets mean and what we can say based on their data. Enghoff and Aldridge (2019) review drug policy related content generated by a range of actors on the online space, from people who consume, supply or produce illicit drugs, websites and various state and civil society organisations. Their work finds enormous value in drawing on these resources to be able to inform and understand our knowledge about drug policy. Although beset by limitations, and various ethical challenges, the work highlights a number of different approaches to research drug policy using these (often novel) online sources to 'illustrate their valuable drug policy insights not possible using more traditional data sources' (Enghoff & Aldridge, 2019, p. 1).

Their work goes beyond just studying cryptomarket use, and includes a review of a range of people who generate online data, from forums of drug users ('the "textbook" example of hard to reach population' – p. 3) to agencies and civil society groups that provide information on policy positions and agency activities, and many of the methods that they outline can be undertaken with little more specialist knowledge than basic (though systematically rigorous) internet usage skills. When focussing on cryptomarket activity, however, the paper highlights the need for more complicated methodologies and complex data to be able to uncover the nature of the illicit drug trade, along with 'encouraging interdisciplinary collaborations that enable new directions for drug policy research less confined to disciplinary silos' (Enghoff & Aldridge, 2019, p. 6). We think it is important to add another factor to these complications – the theoretical positioning of the work that is being conducted.

The utility of these theoretical positions can be shown by two pieces of work, the first of which incorporates both a mixed method approach and a theoretical position. Ladegaard (2017c) tested deterrence theory, essentially whether punishment deters crime, in the digital space of cryptomarkets. Drawing on digital trace data from two markets, news reports related to cryptomarkets along with qualitatively analysed forum data, the work investigated how increased media attention on the markets effected trade, finding that reports were linked to increased revenue, and the conviction/sentencing of Ulbricht (and surrounding news exposure) significantly increasing it. The implication, 'that law enforcement's public relations work and publicized intelligence operations failed to lift actors' subjective perception of risk, and ultimately did not deter trade' (Ladegaard, 2017c, p. 428) if based solely on the digital trace revenue analysis would perhaps have failed to account for who the sentencing was aimed at deterring: market administration team members (i.e. people fulfilling similar roles as Ulbricht) could be turned away from participation while simultaneously revenues could rise based on increases in the number of buyers, who perceive the deterrence as not relevant to their activity. The qualitative analysis of the forum data, however, triangulates the claim and proves an excellent demonstration of processes of neutralisation (Sykes & Matza, 1957) amongst the administrative members of the cryptomarket community and leave the paper making a well justified claim.

The second paper is the aforementioned Cunliffe et al. (2017) (Section 3.4.1) investigation of Australian cryptomarket drug trading. The risk and prices framework (Reuter & Kleiman, 1986) was used to explain and offer an explanation for the particularly large price disparity between online methamphetamine and street level prices that only occurred in this one market out of the five investigated. The paper offered three intertwined possible reasons for this prices difference being apparent: (1) the involvement of dangerous outlaw motorcycle gangs in the supply chain; (2) the high level of attention from law enforcement on this particular product and; (3) the structural characteristics of the street level methamphetamine market – all of which increased the risks of the street methamphetamine dealing, but were absent on cryptomarkets. Of course, these three mechanisms could not be uncovered directly from the findings of the work, but by placing them in a wider context and drawing on a range of drug policy experts, these possible explanations could be deduced and offer directions for further analytical work – both within cryptomarkets research ('do price differentials between street and online prices always occur in dangerous drug markets?') and for drug policy more generally ('is the Australian methamphetamine market really that dangerous?').

3.4.3. The Ever-present Issue of Ethics (and Law Enforcement)

The ethical dimensions of any research should be a central concern, and research in the cryptomarket environment is no different though presents a range of particularly pressing issues. Cryptomarket research, for the main, is a form of internet research – a relatively new domain of investigation that brings its own challenges that are set slightly apart from the traditional ethical procedures that have been in development since the Nuremburg Code of 1949 (Eynon, Fry, &

Schroeder, 2008). A further complication is that, as highlighted earlier in this chapter, cryptomarket research is often conducted by cross-disciplinary teams, and as made clear earlier in the book, cryptomarket activity is not constrained to one particular jurisdiction and there are similarly no geographical constraints on the teams put together to investigate the phenomena (although this holds for numerous research activities). Therefore, it is not always clear cut which professional body's rules should be adhered to (such as the Australian Research council, the UK Economic and Social Research Council, the American Sociological Association, The National Committee for Research Ethics in the Social Sciences and the Humanities in Norway etc.) or which institutional governing structure (Institutional Review Boards in the US, Human Subject Review Boards in Australia or ethical review committees in the UK – again, the list goes on) should be relevant authority to grant permission.

In keeping with Eynon et al. (2008) it is impossible in this limited space 'to cover all of the issues in research ethics; that would require a whole book' and this work will point to some of the main debates only. The three central tenants of confidentiality, anonymity and informed consent still apply as the very foundation of ethical research, but their expression and intricacies require a nuanced understanding in the digital cryptomarket world. Barratt and Maddox's (2016) reflection on their engagement with stigmatised communities of illicit drug purchasers through digital ethnography serves as an excellent overview of the steps that the researchers had to go through to meet these challenges, and also how they protected themselves and their participants from any unintended harms. The paper details how they: prepared for the field work including technical, ethical-legal and social sensitivities; how they engaged with their participants during the fieldwork and were open about their identities – a point they justify in contrast with the perspective of Gehl (2016); the technological issues they faced and how they adapted to a changing environment; and 'after completion of data collection, strategies relating to ethical conduct, technological affordances and community connection continued to inform collaboration surrounding the production, sharing and dissemination of research findings' (Barratt & Maddox, 2016, p. 709). The authors are explicit in their hope that 'this workflow may assist other researchers to emulate, test and adapt our approach to the diverse range of illicit studies online' (Barratt & Maddox, 2016, p. 701).

In traditional research ethics considerations, levels of confidentiality are often tied to concerns as to whether the setting in which an interchange took place was public or private. A personal conversation in a closed room would, in most cases, be considered a private setting – as would a personal conversation in a public space such as a café, and in these cases, anonymity would be a paramount concern. Anonymity would only generally be broken if the setting in which something happened was undeniably a public event (and even then, some researchers may err on the side of caution and obfuscate identity). In internet research, and cryptomarket research is no different, these debates are not as clear cut. Forums are often engaged with pseudonymously and their content can be seen by almost anyone (maybe with an account etc.). These considerations are non-trivial and Eynon et al. (2008) state that the context within which any exchange takes place must be considered and the expectation of the person producing the material, and the place that is deposited, needs to be in mind. This applies to cryptomarket research whether using forum data or cryptomarket digital trace direct from the markets. Décary-Hétu and Aldridge (2015) spend time considering this question with relation to market activity, and 'turn to the norms of the virtual community itself for guidance', concluding that 'these markets explicitly espouse "crypto-anarchist" and radical libertarian principles, leading us [...] to conclude these particular communities would have viewed their content as public' (Décary-Hétu & Aldridge, 2015, p. 133).

Martin and Christin (2016), to date, have provided the most thorough treatment of the ethics in cryptomarket research. Their article reaches beyond being constrained to one particular methodology and they attempt to cover ground common and specific to a range of different approaches. They split internet research into four domains – the ethics of the academy, the researcher, the researched and the institution – and consider different perspective and issues within each. For instance, when discussing the ethics of the researcher, Martin recounts being asked to speak to police officers about the threat of cryptomarkets, but 'declined in favor [*sic.*] of providing a more nuanced perspective regarding the potential harm reduction benefits associated with the growth of the online drugs trade' (Martin & Christin, 2016, p. 87). The second half of the paper dwells more on the data collection/ digital trace methodology and the burden that collecting this data places on both the markets and the Tor network more generally, whether data should be shared and the problems of doing so, including accidental de-anonymisation of people who unintentionally disclose identifying information. Their solution here is that it again depends on context and individual opinion (of the researcher), but argue that data should be made available in a way that minimises the risk of any disclosure by retracting certain fields or delaying release as Christin (2013) sketches as a solution – but acknowledge that this is not a universally held view (cf Branwen's un-redacted scrapes described earlier in Section 3.3.4 that are deposited for all to use).

In their discussion the issues of risks to researchers in collecting data (at the time of collection: minimal) they question how they should deal with the prospect of law enforcement intervention (again, minimal as cryptomarkets are essentially public domains and US law enforcement agencies have demonstrated that they too are monitoring these spaces – see Chapter 1) and weigh up the pros and cons of whether discussing cryptomarkets *at all* could increase law enforcement action against them. Their conclusions are clear – leaving the field of debate is not an option as it could end in misleading information about the dark web causing moral panics, as indeed was the case with the closure and FBI-reported scale of *Silk Road*. More generally, it seems relatively apparent that the broad ethos of ethical guidance implies that the researcher should do as little as possible to disturb the ecosystem that they are studying, and given that the varied participants in cryptomarket action are almost by definition engaged in illicit behaviour, it seems to follow that the best ethical course is not to aid law enforcement do their particular job. However, as Martin and Christin (2016) note, this is very much the concern of the researcher's personal ethics, and the perspective outlined here merely seems the most appropriate to us.

3.5. METHODOLOGICAL SUMMARY

The pace with which cryptomarket research methodologies have developed has been rapid – Barratt's (2012) first missive on the subject was published just seven years ago and in that time frame a range of approaches have been deployed to understand a wide variety of factors about cryptomarkets. Initial works produced during the emergence phase[5] of the cryptomarket paradigm that tried to simply understand the basics of the environment, with those produced during the reconfiguration period similarly trying to understand the impact that the period of uncertainty would bring to the system. During the current epoch, the settlement period, these initial methods have quickly been joined by increasingly complex and thorough approaches that are starting to uncover aspects of both how cryptomarkets function and what this means for other domains of inquiry, and these developments have occurred in a remarkably short amount of time. There is still work to be done, further sophistication of approach (both quantitative and qualitative), triangulation of approaches to work out the weaknesses of any one methodology and the addition of theoretical positioning to the researcher's armoury will help move cryptomarket research forward. Despite the general settled nature of the overarching ecosystem characterised by what we call the third epoch of the cryptomarket domain, the researcher must be ever aware of the changing nature of the specific markets, forums and connected websites/sources of information. Given the arguments laid out in Chapter 1, the hypothesised continuation of their existence in much the same form as they are now, even given recent external shocks and perhaps with a slight change in their role in the drugs trade, these sources of information should continue to provide a solid basis for a wide knowledge as time moves on.

Cryptomarket scholarship is distinguished by a high degree of interdisciplinarity across a variety subjects as well as broad international participation, and there are some themes to this research that come through and are worth delimiting. A central theme in the scholarship has dealt with *harm reduction* and drug use in a broad sense. Researchers have been interested in how cryptomarkets affect fundamental harms associated with drug markets and consumption, namely violence (Barratt, Ferris, et al., 2016; Martin, 2014b, 2014a), drug usage patterns and practices (Aldridge et al., 2018; Bancroft, 2017; Barratt, Lenton, et al., 2016; Mounteney et al., 2017; van der Gouwe, Rigter, & Brunt, 2018), as well as purity and quality (Caudevilla, Ventura, Fornís, et al., 2016). Work within this domain has been situated in the drug policy domain and used both qualitative and quantitative, particularly survey, methods. The *International Journal of Drug Policy* has published a large portion of articles within this domain.

Another branch of the cryptomarket literature may be conceived of as studying the cultural aspects of cryptomarkets. Within this domain, researchers have concerned themselves with culturally embedded meanings of drug purity (Bancroft & Reid, 2016), cryptomarket economics and technology (Bancroft & Scott Reid, 2017; Masson & Bancroft, 2018), and the nature of interactions between cryptomarket participants. Political ideology, and the community of buyers and vendors, have also received great interest (Maddox et al., 2016; Munksgaard and Demant, 2016; Pace, 2017; Sotirakopoulos, 2017; Zajácz, 2017). This is a cultural approach, drawing on cultural studies, sociology and anthropology, which has relied on qualitative methods, namely ethnography and participant observation of forums. In the broader dark web context, Gehl's (2016, 2018) work on the dark web also overlaps with this research theme.

On the economics of cryptomarkets, researchers have examined market changes, composition, supply and demand at a broad level, particularly the transnational dimensions of cryptomarket trade (Aldridge & Décary-Hétu, 2016; Demant, Munksgaard, Décary-Hétu, et al., 2018; Demant, Munksgaard, & Houborg, 2018; Soska & Christin, 2015). This strain of research has remained largely descriptive but is complimented by a more theoretically driven approach by, amongst others, Hardy and Norgaard, (2015), Przepiorka et al. (2017), and Paquet-Clouston et al., (2018), who have approached cryptomarkets from a more theoretically grounded perspective, emphasising subjects like the valuation of drugs and market order. This domain is marked by its use of quantitative data collected through webcrawling, and the participation by sociologists, criminologists, and economists.

A fourth theme has approached social and economic action, market behaviour and cryptomarket transactions drawing on both criminology and sociology. Areas of interest have been the criminological concept of informal social control, conflict management absent of formal law (Morselli et al., 2017), predation and fraud (Moeller et al., 2017), risk (Aldridge & Askew, 2017; Décary-Hétu et al., 2016), and analyses that have focused on institutions and economic action (Bakken et al., 2018; Tzanetakis, 2018b; Tzanetakis et al., 2016). This strand of research has in particular tried to draw comparisons between the organisation and behaviours of illicit drug markets and cryptomarkets, stressing themes such as the absence of violence as a means of social control, fraud, predation, and combined these with criminological and economic sociological concepts. A growing body of literature which has treated more classical criminological topics, namely the displacement of illegal activity following law enforcement intervention, might also be grouped under this theme (e.g. Décary-Hétu & Giommoni, 2017; Ladegaard, 2017a, 2017b).

NOTES

1. Using the search terms 'crypto*market*' and '*market* AND dark*net AND drug*' on both websites, results combined.

2. For example, 'One Gram of COCAINE Coke 1G ABOVE 75% SMOOTH' or '3.5 g (1/8 th) of Grand Daddy Purple Haze'.

3. For example, 'We have sourced some solid skunk bud from one of our suppliers. It is big heavy dense bud, the opposite to our light fluffy Jack Flash ONLY IN TERMS OF DENSITY NOT POTENCY!!, some prefer this type of big bad nugget. Each to their own I say. Head of road testing loves it! ha ha...... @%## Value for coin and a nice heavy stoned guaranteed!! It mulls up to heaps, very skunky and smooth, No leaf No stems No sticks Chronic smell!

We rate it! So far we have received very positive feed back. Give her a go and please let us know what you think'.

4. This is not always the case. On Silk Road 3.1 and Berlusconi Market, for instance, each review is associated with a product and a price. It also has an amount *in-text* which is the sum total of the transaction.

5. See Section 1.1 for a discussion around the emergence, reconfiguration and settlement epochs of cryptomarkets.

4

CHARTING THE UNKNOWN AND FUTURE DIRECTIONS

4.1. SCOPE

In the preceding chapters, we have provided a history of the cryptomarket as a social institution, detailed the cryptomarket economy and the growing academic literature, outlined the methodological approaches of researchers within this domain, and discussed the ethical challenges with which they contend. In this concluding chapter, we proceed to give our best predictions, anchored in the existing research, as to how we conceive the immediate future of cryptomarkets. Some of these are, unavoidably, speculative. It is not our intention to define with complete certainty what will happen, but rather to offer some plausible scenarios and likely trends. The sections below are therefore intended to provide some conceptual grounding for future research into what we believe are important and underdeveloped research areas and are followed by a summary of our predictions and concluding remarks.

4.2. WHERE TO NOW?

4.2.1. Continued Growth and Platform Stability

Since 2011, we have witnessed a relatively stable ecosystem of cryptomarkets emerge on the dark web. These have shown themselves resilient towards both external pressures from law enforcement as well as internal pressures like marketplace exit scams (Barratt & Aldridge, 2016; Décary-Hétu & Giommoni, 2017; Moeller et al., 2017; Soska & Christin, 2015). Dire predictions about the end of the dark web drugs trade, usually made by law enforcement representatives following a short-lived success in disrupting market operations, have proven inaccurate (Power, 2019). Indeed, we expect that there will be no widescale collapse of cryptomarket drug trading, except in the event of a large-scale regulatory intervention against cryptocurrencies or the undermining of Tor's hidden services, both of which seem unlikely after eight years of no such thing.

On the contrary, we predict that the current trends towards further growth of cryptomarket drug trading will continue, despite ongoing threats emanating from both within and outside of the market ecosystem. Similarly, we predict that cryptomarkets will continue to thrive in their current form. As we argued in Chapter 1, it seems that this 'way of doing business' has settled and that rather than any radical reconfigurations imagined during the chaos following Silk Road, the cryptomarkets of today will continue to operate in much the same way as sites from earlier epochs, using Tor and cryptocurrencies, offering escrow and so forth. Given the ongoing success of this formula, and its evident appeal and familiarity amongst a growing number of vendors, purchasers and administrators, there seems to be no great appetite for change, and we therefore expect that further growth will be amongst cryptomarkets that are, for all intents and purposes, identical to Silk Road.

4.2.2. Increasing Localisation

While the expansion of cryptomarket-facilitated drug trading looks set to continue, we do anticipate some change in how this growth manifests. Specifically, we predict that there will be a continuing increase in the proportion of domestic and regional trading at the expense of international/inter-regional transactions. As discussed at some length in Chapters 1 and 2, this trend towards localisation is already evident, and is the result of two concurrent processes: (1) the growing preference on larger, international cryptomarkets for traders to conduct transactions within their home regions/countries (due to increased convenience, less risk crossing borders, etc.) (Aldridge & Askew, 2017; Cunliffe et al., 2017; Demant, Munksgaard, Décary-Hétu, et al., 2018; Martin, 2014b; Van Buskirk, Naicker, et al., 2016); and (2) the steadily increasing number of smaller, particularly non-English language cryptomarkets that cater exclusively to single countries or regions (Nurmi et al., 2017). The latter of these processes is the least well understood, and further research will be needed to understand how non-English language cryptomarkets are used and fit into the broader market ecosystem, for example, with regard to user migration between sites in the event of market takedowns.

Despite our currently limited understanding of non-English language cryptomarkets, we anticipate that there will be an increase in cryptomarket usage outside of those English-speaking regions which currently dominate the trade as internet adoption increases around the world. As discussed in Chapter 2, the moderating factor in country-wide utilisation of cryptomarkets appears to be the unequal distribution of access to Information and Communications Technology (ICT) and associated skills. This is consistent with the cryptomarket literature that posits that ICT access and skills pose a barrier to cryptomarket adoption and utilisation (Demant, Munksgaard, Décary-Hétu, et al., 2018; Martin, 2014b), and that successfully navigating the complexities inherent to cryptomarket usage requires a relatively high degree of knowledge and self-reliance (Kowalski et al., 2019). We suspect that the surplus of 'how to' guides available in English on cryptomarket discussion forums helps entrench the dominance of English-speaking populations, and that the relative deficit in access to specialised cryptomarket knowledge will need to be overcome before cryptomarket usage increases amongst non-English speaking populations.

4.2.3. A Natural Limit?

Cryptomarkets have grown remarkably in the few short years since their inception. However, there inevitability must be a level at which market saturation occurs and growth ceases, a point which we term the 'natural limit'. What factors will eventually determine the natural limit to cryptomarket adoption within a given country? There seems to be at least three answers to this question: Firstly, not all drug users are either capable of, or inclined to, source drugs from a cryptomarket (Bancroft, 2017). Itinerant drug users and those lacking in necessary ICT skills, for example, are unlikely to purchase drugs from a cryptomarket (though it is, of course, possible that their own suppliers may be sourcing from a cryptomarket). Secondly, not all types of drug use are amenable to cryptomarket supply. Spontaneous and unplanned drug use must be facilitated by an immediately accessible dealer, rather than a cryptomarket vendor from whom drugs must be sent via the post which necessarily involves advanced planning and delays measured in days at the very least (Søgaard, Kolind, Haller, & Hunt, 2019). Lastly, for many users sourcing drugs from a cryptomarket may simply not be as convenient compared to accessing a physically proximate dealer (Kowalski et al., 2019; Moyle et al., 2019). This means that, even amongst people who sometimes use cryptomarkets to source drugs, there are likely to remain instances when purchases will be made in-person from local dealers. In combination, these factors will ensure that there remains a thriving – even dominant – inter-personal drugs trade even as cryptomarket usage continues to assume a greater proportion of the illicit drug economy as a whole.

4.2.4. Crackdowns, Volatility and External Shocks

We argued in Section 1.5.3 that the repertoire of law enforcement tactics has expanded to include a dimension of intended deterrence aimed at the wider cryptomarket ecosystem instead of just individual markets, and that the seizure of DeepDotWeb and closure of Reddit forums dedicated to cryptomarkets have complimented the strategy of seizing cryptomarkets. Research has predominantly focused on seizures and their implications for user communities (Ladegaard, 2017a; Munksgaard & Demant, 2016) and displacement following seizures (Décary-Hétu & Giommoni, 2017; Ladegaard, 2019; Van Buskirk et al., 2017). However, the impact of these new strategies, whether implemented by law enforcement or private actors like Reddit, have yet to be explored in depth. Given the importance of knowledge in facilitating access to cryptomarkets discussed in the section above, we suspect that the cracking down on sources of relevant information on the clear web has the potential to significantly slow cryptomarket growth.

In Section 1.5, a question was left open as to the usage of alternative cryptocurrencies, so-called altcoins, and to some extent this has started to be seen on the markets. At one end, Libertas Market only allowed the use of Monero, while others like Dream accepted Bitcoin Cash and Monero in addition to Bitcoin. We suggest that the integration of altcoins on cryptomarkets will continue as new currencies come online, gain prominence and offer technical advantages that the traditional Bitcoin does not, such as increased levels of anonymity (Zcash and Monero), faster processing (Bitcoin Cash, Litecoin), or the ability to deal with more than just a ledger system (Ethereum with its currency Ether). However, the US dollar value of these, and indeed of Bitcoin itself, can be extremely volatile (see Fig. 4.1). This poses unique problems to vendors in particular, who are forced to grapple with macro-economic trends which can severely impact the profitability of their enterprises. The adoption and use of altcoins, as well as the implications of cryptocurrency volatility remain unexplored in the cryptomarket literature.

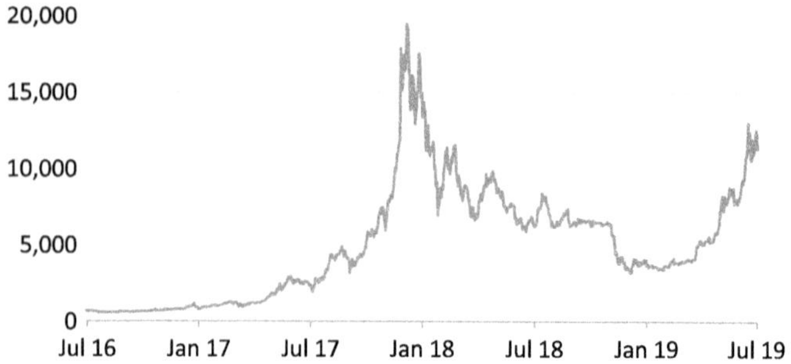

Fig. 4.1. US Dollar Value of Bitcoin, July 2016 to July 2019.

Source: coinmarketcap.com

What we term *external shocks* are factors external to cryptomarkets that influence their functioning. External shocks may be a continual presence that has persisted over a long time (such as Bitcoin volatility) or may appear as radically new developments, such as law enforcement taking control of Hansa Marketplace or the seizure of DeepDotWeb. As law enforcement and other government actions (whether nationally or internationally coordinated), and private companies/ websites become more aware of and reactive to the cryptomarket trade, it seems that external shocks are likely to increase in frequency, and that their impact will correspondingly constitute important areas for future research.

4.2.5. Increasing Intersection with Other Drug Markets

There is growing agreement in the literature that cryptomarkets are having their greatest impact in the 'last mile' of drug trafficking, that is, amongst relatively low-level suppliers located in countries or regions in which consumption takes place (Aldridge & Décary-Hétu, 2016; Demant, Munksgaard, Décary-Hétu, et al., 2018; Dittus et al., 2017). At this point, drugs purchased on cryptomarkets enter the offline market with a range of potential implications. These span from the diffusion of drugs, in terms of drug type, quality and purity, from cryptomarkets to offline markets, to changing patterns of consumption (Aldridge et al., 2018; Barratt et al., 2014; Barratt, Ferris, et al., 2016), and changes to the structure and organisation of illicit drug markets as they exist outside cryptomarkets (Demant, Munksgaard, Décary-Hétu, et al., 2018; Martin, 2014b, 2014a; Martin et al., 2018a). We expect this integration with offline drug markets to continue and intensify as the cryptomarket drugs trade grows further, which will increasingly impact participants in offline drug markets, whether consumers or suppliers.

Section 4.2.1 argued that we are likely to see an increase in the regionalisation of cryptomarkets, and by extension, we are unlikely to see cryptomarkets in their current form disrupting high-level, large-scale established drug importation. However, it seems likely that cryptomarkets will continue becoming increasingly intertwined with mid-level drug supply (Aldridge & Décary-Hétu, 2016), as evidenced by the high-profile arrest of the German cryptomarket vendor *Shiny Flakes* (see Locker, 2015). There has also been a noted increase in the use of social media for drug dealing (Bakken & Demant, 2019; Demant et al., 2019; Moyle et al., 2019; Stevens, 2016), which exists at the same levels of the drug trade on cryptomarkets in that both require some level of engagement with computerised systems, and it is reasonable to expect an increasing overlap at this level (i.e. sourcing supply on cryptomarkets and then reselling through social media).

We predict that cryptomarkets are also likely to play an increasing role in social supply (Chatwin & Potter, 2014; Parker, Aldridge, & Measham, 1998; Potter, 2009) and 'minimally commercial supply' (Coomber & Moyle, 2014) whereby a member(s) of a group of friends or acquaintances goes to the effort to understand and purchase products from a cryptomarket with the intention of 'sorting out' a group, for minimal or no profit (Kowalski et al., 2019). There is, as of yet, scant evidence of social media/cryptomarket reseller patterns and little by the way of social/minimal commercial supply beyond journalistic reports of specific cases (see, e.g., Clarke-Billings, 2018). Such an overlap gains relevance for the discussion of organised crime and cryptomarkets because the circumvention of organised crime groups which earlier cryptomarket studies hypothesised could manifest through direct producer-buyer relations (Martin, 2014b, 2014a), may instead manifest through social media and small-scale dealers sourcing their supply from the digital world, rather than relying on conventional drug distribution channels, with a subsequent effect being the availability of a wider range of drugs in regions not typically associated with their consumption (such as in Ewens, 2018).

4.2.6. Increased Offending Due to Exposure to Other Illicit Goods and Services

As detailed in Chapter 1, the period following the fall of Silk Road was accompanied by a gradual yet increasing overlap between cryptomarkets and the stolen data economy. These disparate observations suggest that the cryptomarket should not be approached as an isolated market, but rather as an integrated and developing part of different illicit markets. While originally distinct from the 'cryptomarket scene', the market for stolen data increasingly overlaps with the market for illicit drugs (Soska & Christin, 2015). Given the stability of this pattern, particularly in large markets such as Alphabay and Evolution which both had long-established ties to carding communities, it is unlikely that this overlap is a temporary phase. This subject is, in comparison to the distribution of illicit drugs, relatively unexamined on cryptomarkets and mainly studied in the context of carding forums and communities (e.g. Hutchings, 2014; Hutchings & Holt, 2017). Whether the integration between stolen data and illicit drugs markets will continue or deepen is presently unknown, as are the current and future implications of these trends. However, we propose that a question worthy of further investigation is whether people who use cryptomarkets are engaging in more varied forms of offending as a result of their exposure to other illicit goods and services hosted on these sites.

4.2.7. Gentrification

While cryptomarkets may be exposing users to a wider range of drugs and crimes than would otherwise be the case, it is also possible that by removing face-to-face interactions between customers and dealers, cryptomarkets are creating an online milieu that feels qualitatively less 'criminal' in favour of one that is, in our words, more 'gentrified'. The gentrification hypothesis posits that the unique processes and dynamics that are associated with cryptomarket drug trading, particularly anonymity and geographical separation between buyers and sellers, result in prosocial changes in individual behaviours and experiences, shared norms and interactions, and, ultimately, in the personal identities of market participants in comparison to those involved in other forms of illicit drug exchange (Martin, 2018). These dynamics, in turn, attract people whose values are in greater alignment with the prosocial norms we propose are prevalent on cryptomarkets, thereby further entrenching the gentrification process.

From a customer perspective, acquiring drugs via a cryptomarket is a markedly different experience from any other method, for example, purchasing from a stranger at a site of drug consumption or even from a known dealer visiting one's private residence (Masson & Bancroft, 2018; Van Hout & Bingham, 2013b, 2014). Relevant differences include the constant maintenance of physical separation between buyers and sellers which, operating in tandem with third-party dispute resolution mechanisms hosted on cryptomarkets, limit the possibility of violence, intimidation and other exploitative interactions, whether initiated from either party. Cryptomarkets also offer customers an unprecedented variety of choice of drugs and suppliers, which creates fierce (though non-violent) competition amongst vendors for customer attention and patronage (Bakken et al., 2018). According to the qualitative evidence available (Masson & Bancroft, 2018; Van Hout & Bingham, 2013b, 2014), the competition between vendors in this 'buyer's market' manifests in unusually high levels of customer service.

On cryptomarkets, it appears that customers are often treated as just that – customers – replete with much of the service, support and customer-is-always-right deference one may typically encounter in the legal retailing economy. The pre-cryptomarket experience of buying drugs in a shady car-park or back alley is replaced in favour of yet another customisable online shopping experience, replete with internal search engines, reviews and ratings, FAQs, express door-to-door delivery, and 24/7 customer support. While transgression and the thrill of temporary engagement with the criminal underworld may still be experienced ordering drugs using a computer as when doing so in-person, questions remain as to how the cryptomarket 'shopping experience', marked by differences in the form of valued patronage, lowered risk of arrest, and reduced potential for violence and other negative interactions, shape customers' perceptions of their own offending and participation in the illicit drug economy.

While the customer experience on cryptomarkets arguably represents a gentrified alternative to purchasing drugs via inter-personal means, how do these processes affect vendors? From the supplier perspective, we propose that selling drugs via a cryptomarket is even more likely to be characterised by gentrification than it is for customers. Much of this difference, we suggest, concerns vendor perceptions of risk. Drug retailing in its conventional, offline forms is widely recognised as the most risky stage of the distribution process (Bouchard & Ouellet, 2011). This is because dealers are exposed not only to the risk of arrest from drug investigators and undercover operatives, but also because customers themselves can be dangerous – either as potential robbers or as informers to the authorities. In addition, drug dealers are exposed to the risk of violent predation from competitors as well as 'stand over men' and organised crime groups looking to prey upon those who, by virtue of the illegality of their work, remain outside the protection of the state. While one should be mindful that risk of violence in conventional drug markets is often less than is commonly supposed (Coomber & Maher, 2006), we argue that there remains a significant psychological gulf between dealing that involves relatively low risk of violence, and that which involves *practically no risk*, as currently appears to be the case when selling drugs via cryptomarkets.

Given these differences in risk and the non-violent but intensely competitive online trading environment, we propose that one of the main implications of the growth of cryptomarkets is the creation of a new type of drug dealer – the cryptomarket vendor – whose motivations, skillsets, and daily experiences of their work are likely to vary considerably from those involved in other types of dealing. With the risk of violence and customer informants effectively eliminated, and the risk of arrest by law enforcement likely to be significantly lower than is the case for those engaging in inter-personal forms of drug dealing, we speculate that cryptomarket vendors are free to focus on the development of working identities that are marked by professionalism, brand creation and entrepreneurialism. Online anonymity also offers the prospect of decoupling one's personal identity and work as a drug supplier in a way that is not typically available to other types of drug dealing. This helps insulate cryptomarket vendors from some of the seductions as well as dangers of offline dealing, such as having street credibility to gain and defend, as well as risks of predatory violence and arrest. Instead, different capacities are needed for success for those involved in cryptomarket vending, including ICT knowledge, customer service and marketing skills.

4.2.8. Harm Reduction

As discussed in Chapter 2, harm reduction constitutes an important component of contemporary cryptomarket research, and that there are promising but so far largely unvalidated claims regarding the potential of cryptomarkets to reduce a variety of drug-related harms. Much of the research in this area centres on the role played by discussion forums as centres of knowledge exchange regarding drug potency and adulteration, and safer usage practices (Aldridge et al., 2018; Bancroft, 2017; Barratt, Lenton, et al., 2016; Van Hout & Bingham, 2013a; Van Hout & Hearne, 2017). We suggest that a factor that complicates contemporary assessments of the role of cryptomarket discussion forums in facilitating harm reduction is both the elimination of clear web sources of information, as well as the recent rapid turnover of long-established cryptomarkets. While individual users can migrate from market to market with relative ease (Van Buskirk et al., 2017), we predict that if the recent rapid turnover of cryptomarkets continues the formation of stable communities of users who participate in cryptomarket harm reduction discussion forums will be disrupted. We suspect that this trend will impede the effective exchange of information upon which discussion forums depend, thereby reducing some of the utility of discussion forums in facilitating harm reduction.

4.2.9. A Summary of Predictions

In summation, along with the continued growth of cryptomarkets in much the same format as was originally defined by Silk Road, we expect to observe a continued movement towards localisation and smaller scale markets that do not serve customers across national boundaries. These are likely to fulfil part of the market ecosystem and still leave space for larger markets that reach maturity (see Section 2.1.2) and that will continue to dominate the cryptomarket drugs trade, before being dealt a mortal blow in one way or another (also detailed in Section 2.1.2). We also expect there to be increasingly sophisticated attempts by law enforcement agencies to disrupt the ecosystem through the use of novel approaches that are not necessarily aimed directly at the markets, but rather are aimed at spreading 'FUD' (fear, uncertainty and doubt) through cryptomarkets. Processes external to the cryptomarket system may also play a role in disrupting their function alongside this. While we do not expect a security compromise of the main tools upon which cryptomarkets depend (i.e. Tor, the existence of cryptocurrencies in general, etc.), we do expect issues such as the price volatility of Bitcoin and other related payment currencies to interrupt the ability of vendors and buyers to easily trade.

We further anticipate that there will be no movement away from cryptomarkets offering a range of products outside illicit drugs, such as carding and fraud services. Similarly, we do not expect weapons to disappear in their entirety. We do, however, expect the trade in these other commodities to remain minimal. How the availability of these products and services on the same platform as illicit drugs are likely to interact with cryptomarket sales, however, is complex and raises questions much broader than the study of just internet facilitated drug trading – touching on some of the more pressing issues facing criminology as a whole. We suggest, however, that the role that cryptomarkets will play in facilitating other criminality is likely to be minimal and, in many ways, they can be seen to be reducing violence – gentrifying the drug purchasing experience, even if their utility in promoting some of the harm reduction messages that have been reported on in the past recede.

4.3. CONCLUDING REMARKS

Cryptomarkets are fascinating phenomena. At their most basic, they represent a relatively insignificant part of the global drug economy, and yet they have captured the attention of researchers and the general public alike in ways that are vastly disproportionate to their immediate size. There are several reasons for this. Despite their small size, cryptomarkets are sites of astounding technological and criminal innovation. They represent a bold challenge not only to the forces of prohibition, and law and order, but also to the long-established systems of inter-personal drug exchange and distribution that have dominated this most profitable of black market industries for over a century. As such, they are of particular importance to our home discipline of criminology. Yet the criminal aspect of cryptomarkets only tells us one side of the story. In addition to their exceptional criminological relevance, cryptomarkets are also sites of human interaction and entrepreneurialism that exist outside the realm of state governance and regulation. As such, they hold important lessons beyond the realm of criminology, attracting the attention of economists, health professionals, sociologists, computer scientists and digital ethnographers. We anticipate and welcome the participation and contribution of researchers from even broader disciplines in the years to come (and there is certainly space for anthropologists, social psychologists, linguists and advertising scholars at the very least).

Cryptomarkets are also uniquely visible. Their public prominence online and location outside of legitimate state and commercial enterprise means that researchers across the breadth of the academy can capture and use data contained therein without the approval of jealous corporate or government gatekeepers. This means that, despite their relative novelty, we know much more about cryptomarkets – their composition, their operations, how they develop over time – than we do about the broader illicit markets within which they are embedded. This visibility, and the real-time, granular detail with which cryptomarkets are studied, gives them particular scholarly importance as a testing ground for theories that have long shaped our understanding of how and why people act the way they do, but have too infrequently faced the spotlight of empirical scrutiny. We now have good evidence, for example, that deterrence (at least in online drug markets) is ineffective (Ladegaard, 2017c), and that crime displacement and the Iron Law of Prohibition are real (Ladegaard, 2019; Martin et al., 2018a). Expect more theoretical pins to fall as researchers take advantage of the unprecedented data that are now available.

This chapter, and indeed much of this book, has sought to present cryptomarket research as both a valuable achievement as well as a work in progress. In an astoundingly short space of time, an entirely new online phenomenon has attained a level of increasing importance not only amongst traders of illicit drugs in many parts of the world, but also within the rapidly growing cryptomarket research community. Collectively, we have made a decent start in uncovering the complexities and implications of cryptomarkets and their place in the world, but clearly much remains to be done. More innovation and research, whether empirical, methodological or theoretical needs to be undertaken in order to better understand the phenomenon in front of us today, as well as how it develops in the years to come. We look forward to seeing how this unfolds!

BIBLIOGRAPHY

Afilipoaie, A., & Shortis, P. (2018). *Crypto-market enforcement – New strategy and tactics*. Technical Report. Global Drug Policy Observatory, Swansea. https://doi.org/10.1016/j.drugpo.2018.01.003.13

AFP. (2017). World congress speech: Global realities of child exploitation. Australian Federal Police. Retreived from https://www.afp.gov.au/news-media/media-releases/speech-global-realities-child-exploitation

Akerlof, G. A. (1970). The market for "lemons" quality uncertainty and the market mechanism. *The Quarterly Journal of Economics*, *84*(3), 488. https://doi.org/10.2307/1879431

Aldridge, J., & Askew, R. (2017). Delivery dilemmas: How drug cryptomarket users identify and seek to reduce their risk of detection by law enforcement. *International Journal of Drug Policy*, *41*(March), 101–109. https://doi.org/10.1016/j.drugpo.2016.10.010

Aldridge, J., & Décary-Hétu, D. (2014). Not an "Ebay for Drugs": The cryptomarket "Silk Road" as a paradigm shifting criminal innovation. *SSRN Electronic Journal*, *564*(October), 29. https://doi.org/10.2139/ssrn.2436643

Aldridge, J., & Décary-Hétu, D. (2015). *Cryptomarkets: The darknet as an online drug market innovation*. Technical Report. University of Manchester, Manchester.

Aldridge, J., & Décary-Hétu, D. (2016). Hidden wholesale: The drug diffusing capacity of online drug cryptomarkets. *International Journal of Drug Policy*, *35*, 7–15. https://doi.org/10.1016/j.drugpo.2016.04.020

Aldridge, J., Stevens, A., & Barratt, M. J. (2018). Will growth in cryptomarket drug buying increase the harms of illicit drugs? *Addiction*, *113*(5), 789–796. https://doi.org/10.1111/add.13899

Aniello, S., & Caneppele, S. (2018). Selling stolen goods on the online markets: An explorative study. *Global Crime*, *19*(1), 42–62. https://doi.org/10.1080/17440572.2017.1418333

Bakken, S. A., & Demant, J. J. (2019). Sellers' risk perceptions in public and private social media drug markets. *International Journal of Drug Policy*. Retrieved from https://doi.org/10.1016/j.drugpo.2019.03.009

Bakken, S. A., Moeller, K., & Sandberg, S. (2018). Coordination problems in cryptomarkets: Changes in cooperation, competition and valuation. *European Journal of Criminology*, *15*(4), 1–19. https://doi.org/10.1177/1477370817749177

Bancroft, A. (2017). Responsible use to responsible harm: Illicit drug use and peer harm reduction in a darknet cryptomarket. *Health, Risk and Society*, *19*(7–8), 336–350.

Bancroft, A., & Reid, P. S. (2016). Concepts of illicit drug quality among darknet market users: Purity, embodied experience, craft and chemical knowledge. *International Journal of Drug Policy*, *35*, 42–49.

Bancroft, A., & Scott Reid, P. (2017). Challenging the techno-politics of anonymity: The case of cryptomarket users. *Information, Communication & Society*, *20*(4), 497–512.

Barbrook, R., & Cameron, A. (2001). Californian ideology. In P. Ludlow (Ed.), *Crypto anarchy, cyberstates and pirate utopias* (Kindle edition). Cambridge, MA: MIT Press.

Barlow, J. P. (2001). A declaration of the independence of cyberspace. In P. Ludlow (Ed.), *Crypto anarchy, cyberstates and pirate utopias* (Kindle edition). Cambridge, MA: MIT Press.

Barratt, M. J. (2011). Discussing illicit drugs in public internet forums: Visibility, stigma, and pseudonymity. In *Proceedings of the 5th international conference on communities and technologies* (pp. 159–168).

Barratt, M. J. (2012). Silk Road: eBay for drugs. *Addiction*, *107*(3), 683–683. https://doi.org/10.1111/j.1360-0443.2011.03709.x

Barratt, M. J., & Aldridge, J. (2016). Everything you always wanted to know about drug cryptomarkets* (*but were afraid to ask). *International Journal of Drug Policy*, *35*, 1–6. https://doi.org/10.1016/j.drugpo.2016.07.005

Barratt, M. J., Ferris, J. A., & Winstock, A. R. (2014). Use of Silk Road, the online drug marketplace, in the United Kingdom, Australia and the United States. *Addiction*, *109*(5), 774–783. https://doi.org/10.1111/add.12470

Barratt, M. J., Ferris, J. A., & Winstock, A. R. (2016). Safer scoring? Cryptomarkets, social supply and drug market violence. *International Journal of Drug Policy*, *35*, 24–31. https://doi.org/10.1016/j.drugpo.2016.04.019

Barratt, M. J., Ferris, J. A., Zahnow, R., Palamar, J. J., Maier, L. J., & Winstock, A. R. (2017). Moving on from representativeness: Testing the utility of the global drug survey. *Substance Abuse: Research and Treatment*, *11*(June), 16391. https://doi.org/10.1177/1178221817716391

Barratt, M. J., Lenton, S., Maddox, A., & Allen, M. (2016). 'What if you live on top of a bakery and you like cakes?' – Drug use and harm trajectories before, during and after the emergence of Silk Road. *International Journal of Drug Policy*, *35*, 50–57. https://doi.org/http://dx.doi.org/10.1016/j.drugpo.2016.04.006

Barratt, M. J., & Maddox, A. (2016). Active engagement with stigmatised communities through digital ethnography. *Qualitative Research*, *16*(6), 701–719. https://doi.org/10.1177/1468794116648766

Barrera, V., Malm, A., Décary-Hétu, D., & Munksgaard, R. (2019). Size and scope of the tobacco trade on the darkweb. *Global Crime*, *20*(1), 26–44.

Beckert, J., & Dewey, M. (2017). Introduction: The social organization of illicit markets. In J. Beckert & M. Dewey (Eds.), *The architecture of illegal markets: Towards an economic sociology of illegality in the economy* (1st ed., pp. 1–36). Oxford: Oxford University Press.

Beckert, J., & Wehinger, F. (2013). In the shadow: Illegal markets and economic sociology. *Socio-Economic Review*, *11*(1), 5–30. https://doi.org/10.1093/ser/mws020

Bergman, M. K. (2001). White paper: The deep web: Surfacing hidden value. *The Journal of Electronic Publishing*, *7*(1). https://doi.org/10.3998/3336451.0007.104

Berry, M. (2018). Technology and organised crime in the smart city: An ethnographic study of the illicit drug trade. *City, Territory and Architecture*, *5*(1), 16. https://doi.org/10.1186/s40410-018-0091-7

Bilgrei, O. R. (2016). From "herbal highs" to the "heroin of cannabis": Exploring the evolving discourse on synthetic cannabinoid use in a Norwegian Internet drug forum. *International Journal of Drug Policy*, *29*(March), 1–8. https://doi.org/10.1016/j.drugpo.2016.01.011

Böhme, R., Christin, N., Edelman, B., & Moore, T. (2015). Bitcoin: Economics, technology, and governance. *Journal of Economic Perspectives*, *29*(2), 213–238. https://doi.org/10.1257/jep.29.2.213

Bond, J.-M. (2017). *How to buy drugs (or anything else) on the deep web*. Austin, TX: The Daily Dot.

Bouchard, M., & Ouellet, F. (2011). "Is small beautiful?" The link between risks and size in illegal drug markets. *Global Crime*, *12*(1), 70–86.

Branwen, G. (2015). Black-market risks. Retrieved from http://www.gwern.net/Black-market survival

Branwen, G. (2017). Darknet market mortality risks. Retrieved from https://www.gwern.net/DNM survival. Accessed on April 10, 2017.

Branwen, G., Christin, N., Décary-Hétu, D., Andersen, R. M., StExo, Presidente, E., ... Goode, S. (2015). Dark net market archives, 2011–2015. Retrieved from www.gwern.net/Black-market archives

Brewster, T. (2017). How the FBI hacked a dark web shopper plotting a mail bomb hit. *Forbes*. Retrieved from https://www.forbes.com/sites/thomasbrewster/2017/06/13/mail-bomb-buyer-busted-on-dark-web/#57b3b141eead

Broséus, J., Rhumorbarbe, D., Mireault, C., Ouellette, V., Crispino, F., & Décary-Hétu, D. (2016). Studying illicit drug trafficking on Darknet markets: Structure and organisation from a Canadian perspective. *Forensic Science International*, *264*, 7–14.

Burns, L., Roxburgh, A., Bruno, R., & Van Buskirk, J. (2014). Monitoring drug markets in the Internet age and the evolution of drug monitoring systems in Australia. *Drug Testing and Analysis*, *6*(7–8), 840–845. https://doi.org/10.1002/dta.1613

Buxton, J., & Bingham, T. (2015). *Policy brief 7: The rise and challenge of dark net drug markets* (p. 24). Swansea: Global Drug Policy Observatory.

Caleb. (2019, May 7). What do we know about the deepdotweb seizure? *Medium*. Retrieved from https://medium.com/@c5/what-do-we-know-about-the-deepdotweb-seizure-98ca45de9987

Caudevilla, F., Ventura, M., Fornís, I., Barratt, M. J., Vidal, C., Lladanosa, C. G., ... Calzada, N. (2016). Results of an international drug testing service for cryptomarket users. *International Journal of Drug Policy*, *35*(March), 38–41. https://doi.org/10.1016/j.drugpo.2016.04.017

Chatwin, C., & Potter, G. (2014). Blurred boundaries: The artificial distinction between "use" and "supply" in the U.K. cannabis market. *Contemporary Drug Problems*, *41*(4), 536–550. https://doi.org/10.1177/0091450914567120

Chaum, D. (1981). Untraceable electronic mail, return addresses, and digital pseudonyms, *Communications*, *24*(2), 84–90.

Chaum, D., Fiat, A., & Naor, M. (1988). Untraceable electronic cash. In *Advances in cryptology – CRYPTO' 88* (pp. 319–327). New York, NY: Springer. https://doi.org/10.1007/0-387-34799-2_25

Chen, A. (2011). The underground website where you can buy any drug imaginable. Retrieved from http://gawker.com/the-underground-website-where-you-can-buy-any-drug-imag-30818160. Accessed on December 10, 2015.

Christin, N. (2013). Traveling the Silk Road: A measurement analysis of a large anonymous online marketplace. In *Proceedings of the 22nd international conference on world wide web* (pp. 213–224). https://doi.org/10.1145/2488388.2488408

Ciccarone, D. (2017). Fentanyl in the US heroin supply: A rapidly changing risk environment. *International Journal of Drug Policy*, *46*, 107–111.

Cimpanu, C. (2018, March 21). Reddit bans community dedicated to dark web markets. *Bleeping Computer*. Retrieved from https://www.bleepingcomputer.com/news/security/reddit-bans-community-dedicated-to-dark-web-markets/

Cimpanu, C. (2019, April). Another dark web marketplace bites the dust – Wall Street Market. *ZDNet*.

Clarke-Billings, L. (2018). Teen who bought MDMA from Dark Web which killed two friends at gig is jailed. *The Mirror*, November 29. Retrieved from https://www.mirror.co.uk/news/uk-news/teen-jailed-over-friends-deaths-13663926

Coomber, R., & Maher, L. (2006). Street-level drug market activity in Sydney's primary heroin markets: Organization, adulteration practices, pricing, marketing and violence. *Journal of Drug Issues*, *36*(3), 719–753.

Coomber, R., & Moyle, L. (2014). Beyond drug dealing: Developing and extending the concept of 'social supply' of illicit drugs to 'minimally commercial supply.' *Drugs: Education, Prevention and Policy*, *21*(2), 157–164. https://doi.org/10.3109/09687637.2013.798265

Coomber, R., & Moyle, L. (2017). The changing shape of street-level heroin and crack supply in England: Commuting, holidaying and cuckooing drug dealers across 'county lines.' *The British Journal of Criminology*, *58*(6), 1323–1342. https://doi.org/10.1093/bjc/azx068

Cox, J. (2016). "Operation hyperion" targets suspected dark web users around the world. *Motherboard*, November 3. Retrieved from http://motherboard.vice.com/read/operation-hyperion-targets-suspected-dark-web-users-around-the-world

Cunliffe, J. D., Décary-Hétu, D., & Pollak, T. A. (2019). Nonmedical prescription psychiatric drug use and the darknet:

A cryptomarket analysis. *International Journal of Drug Policy*. https://doi.org/10.1016/J.DRUGPO.2019.01.016

Cunliffe, J. D., Martin, J., Décary-Hétu, D., & Aldridge, J. (2017). An island apart? Risks and prices in the Australian cryptomarket drug trade. *International Journal of Drug Policy*, *50*, 64–73. https://doi.org/10.1016/j.drugpo.2017.09.005

Cuthbertson, A. (2018). What happens when you spend a week fishing on the dark web? *The Independent*, October 15.

Dark.fail. (2019). dark.fail. Retrieved from https://dark.fail/#philosophy. Accessed on May 17, 2019.

Décary-Hétu, D., & Aldridge, J. (2015). Sifting through the net: Monitoring of online offenders by researchers. *European Review of Organised Crime*, 2(2), 122–141.

Décary-Hétu, D., & Giommoni, L. (2017). Do police crackdowns disrupt drug cryptomarkets? A longitudinal analysis of the effects of operation onymous. *Crime, Law and Social Change*, *67*(1), 55–75. https://doi.org/10.1007/s10611-016-9644-4

Décary-Hétu, D., & Leppänen, A. (2013). Criminals and signals: An assessment of criminal performance in the carding underworld. *Security Journal*, *2939*, 442–460. https://doi.org/10.1057/sj.2013.39

Décary-Hétu, D., Paquet-Clouston, M., & Aldridge, J. (2016). Going international? Risk taking by cryptomarket drug vendors. *International Journal of Drug Policy*, *35*, 69–76. https://doi.org/10.1016/j.drugpo.2016.06.003

Décary-Hétu, D., & Quessy-Doré, O. (2017). Are repeat buyers in cryptomarkets loyal customers? Repeat business between dyads of cryptomarket vendors and users. *American Behavioral Scientist*, *61*(11), 1–17. https://doi.org/10.1177/0002764217734265

DeepDotWeb. (2013a). Sheep marketplace owner just got doxxed?! *DeepDotWeb*, November 30. Retrieved from https://web.archive.org/web/20161008214807/https://www.deepdotweb.com/2013/11/30/sheep-owner-just-got-doxxed/

DeepDotWeb. (2013b). Sheep marketplace scam: Over 40,000,000$ in the biggest darknet scam ever! *DeepDotWeb*, November 30. Retrieved from https://web.archive.org/web/20160519060726/https://www.deepdotweb.com/2013/11/30/sheep-marketplace-scammed-over-40000000-in-the-biggets-darknet-scam-ever/

DeepDotWeb. (2015a). Interview with Valhalla (Silkkitie) admin. *DeepDotWeb*.

DeepDotWeb. (2015b). Evolution market background: Carding forums, ponzi schemes and LE. *DeepDotWeb*, March 18. Retrieved from https://web.archive.org/web/20170712000306/https://www.deepdotweb.com/2015/03/18/evolution-market-background-carding-forums-ponzi-schemes-le/

DeepDotWeb. (2015c). Interview with AlphaBay market admin. *DeepDotWeb*, April.

DeepDotWeb. (2016a). Interview with Oasis market admin. *DeepDotWeb*.

DeepDotWeb. (2016b). Interview with Tochka market admin. *DeepDotWeb*.

DeepDotWeb. (2017a). 176 Investigations started In Sweden, operation hyperion. *Deep Dot Web*, January 6. *DeepDotWeb*. Retrieved from https://web.archive.org/web/20170613052614/https://www.deepdotweb.com/2017/01/06/176-investigations-started-norway-operation-hyperion/

DeepDotWeb. (2017b). Sheep marketplace owner gets nine years in prison. *DeepDotWeb*, October 14. Retrieved from https://web.archive.org/web/20171015054845/https://www.

deepdotweb.com/2017/10/14/sheep-marketplace-owner-gets-nine-years-prison/

DeepDotWeb. (2019). Dream market will permanently suspend operations next month. *DeepDotWeb*. Retrieved from https://web.archive.org/web/20190330123331/https://www.deepdotweb.com/2019/03/29/dream-market-will-permanently-suspend-operations-next-month/

Demant, J., Bakken, S. A., Oksanen, A., & Gunnlaugsson, H. (2019). Drug dealing on Facebook, Snapchat and Instagram: A qualitative analysis of novel drug markets in the Nordic countries. *Drug and Alcohol Review*, *38*(4), 377–385. https://doi.org/10.1111/dar.12932

Demant, J., Munksgaard, R., Décary-Hétu, D., & Aldridge, J. (2018). Going local on a global platform: A critical analysis of the transformative potential of cryptomarkets for organized illicit drug crime. *International Criminal Justice Review*, *28*(3), 255–274. https://doi.org/10.1177/1057567718769719

Demant, J., Munksgaard, R., & Houborg, E. (2018). Personal use, social supply or redistribution? cryptomarket demand on Silk Road 2 and Agora. *Trends in Organized Crime*, *21*(1), 42–61. https://doi.org/10.1007/s12117-016-9281-4

Dhanapala, J., Donowaki, M., & Lumpe, L. (2019). *Small arms control: Old weapons, new issues*. Abingdon: Routledge.

Diekmann, A., Jann, B., Przepiorka, W., & Wehrli, S. (2014). Reputation formation and the evolution of cooperation in anonymous online markets. *American Sociological Review*, *79*(791), 65–85. https://doi.org/10.1177/0003122413512316

Dingledine, R., Syverson, P., Mathewson, N., & Syverson, P. (2004). Tor: The second-generation onion router. Retrieved from http://www.dtic.mil/dtic/tr/fulltext/u2/a465464.pdf

Dittus, M., Wright, J., & Graham, M. (2017). Platform criminalism: The "last-mile" geography of the darknet market supply chain. Preprint. Retrieved from https://arxiv.org/abs/1712.10068

DOJ. (2017). *AlphaBay, the largest online "Dark Market," shut down.* Department of Justice. Retrieved from https://www.justice.gov/opa/pr/alphabay-largest-online-dark-market-shut-down

DOJ. (2018). *Operation darkness falls results in arrest of one of the most prolific dark net Fentanyl Vendors in the World. US Department of Justice.* Retrieved from https://www.justice.gov/opa/pr/operation-darkness-falls-results-arrest-one-most-prolific-dark-net-fentanyl-vendors-world

Dolliver, D. S. (2015). Evaluating drug trafficking on the Tor Network: Silk Road 2, the sequel. *International Journal of Drug Policy*, *26*(11), 1113–1123. https://doi.org/10.1016/j.drugpo.2015.01.008

Dolliver, D. S., & Kenney, J. L. (2016). Characteristics of drug vendors on the Tor network: A cryptomarket comparison. *Victims & Offenders*, *11*(4), 600–620. https://doi.org/10.1080/15564886.2016.1173158

Dupont, B., Côté, A.-M., Boutin, J.-I., & Fernandez, J. (2017). Darkode: Recruitment patterns and transactional features of "the most dangerous cybercrime forum in the world." *American Behavioral Scientist*, *61*(11), 1219–1243. https://doi.org/10.1177/0002764217734263

Duxbury, S. W., & Haynie, D. L. (2017). The network structure of opioid distribution on a darknet cryptomarket. *Journal of Quantitative Criminology*, *34*(4), 921–941. https://doi.org/10.1007/s10940-017-9359-4

Duxbury, S. W., & Haynie, D. L. (2018). Building them up, breaking them down: Topology, vendor selection patterns, and a digital drug market's robustness to disruption. *Social Networks*, *52*, 238–250. https://doi.org/10.1016/j.socnet.2017.09.002

Ehney, R., & Shorter, J. D. (2016). Deep Web, Dark Web, Invisible Web and the Post ISIS world. *Issues in Information Systems*, *17*(4), 36–41.

EMCDDA. (2016). *Recent changes in Europe's MDMA/ecstasy market*. Luxembourg. Retrieved from http://www.emcdda.europa.eu/system/files/publications/2473/TD0116348ENN.pdf

EMCDDA & Europol. (2016). *EU drug markets report. In-depth analysis*. Luxembourg. https://doi.org/10.2810/219411

EMCDDA & Europol. (2017). Drugs and the darknet: Perspectives for enforcement, research and policy. Retrieved from http://www.emcdda.europa.eu/system/files/publications/6585/TD0417834ENN.pdf

Enghoff, O., & Aldridge, J. (2019). The value of unsolicited online data in drug policy research. *International Journal of Drug Policy*, 1–9. https://doi.org/10.1016/j.drugpo.2019.01.023

Espinosa, R. (2019). Scamming and the reputation of drug dealers on darknet markets. *International Journal of Industrial Organization*, in press. https://doi.org/halshs-02180182

EUROPOL. (2016). *Darknet arms vendor arrested in slovenia with support of europol*. The Hague, Netherlands: EUROPOL.

EUROPOL. (2019). *Global law enforcement action against vendors and buyers on the dark web*. The Hague, Netherlands: EUROPOL. Retrieved from https://www.europol.europa.eu/newsroom/news/global-law-enforcement-action-against-vendors-and-buyers-dark-web

Ewens, H. (2018). How Xanax became the British teenager's drug of choice. *VICE*, January 26.

Retrieved from www.vice.com/en_uk/article/ne4mvb/how-british-teens-got-hooked-on-xanax

Eynon, R., Fry, J., & Schroeder, R. (2008). The ethics of online research. In *The SAGE handbook of online research methods* (pp. 19–37). London: SAGE Publications Ltd. https://doi.org/10.4135/9781473957992.n2

Fanselow, F. S. (1990). The bazaar economy or how bizarre is the bazaar really? *Man*, *25*(2), 250–265.

Finn, M. A., & Stalans, L. J. (2016). How targeted enforcement shapes marketing decisions of pimps: Evidence of displacement and innovation. *Victims & Offenders*, *11*(4), 1–22.

Foley, S., Karlsen, J. R., & Putniņš, T. J. (2019). Sex, drugs, and bitcoin: How much illegal activity is financed through cryptocurrencies? *The Review of Financial Studies*, *32*(5), 1798–1853. https://doi.org/10.1093/rfs/hhz015

Fonhof, A., van der Bruggen, M., & Takes, F. (2018). Characterizing key players in child exploitation networks on the dark net. In *International conference on complex networks and their applications* (pp. 412–423). Springer.

Frost, A. (2019). Fentanyl on dark web. *Herald Sun*, May 5.

GDS. (2018). *Global Drug Survey 2018*.

Gehl, R. W. (2016). Power/freedom on the dark web: A digital ethnography of the Dark Web social network. *NewMedia & Society*, *18*(7), 1219–1235. https://doi.org/10.1177/1461444814554900

Gehl, R. W. (2018). *Weaving the dark web: Legitimacy on Freenet, Tor, and I2P* (1st ed.). Cambridge, MA: MIT Press.

Goldsmith, J. (2000). Unilateral regulation of the Internet: A modest defence. *European Journal of International Law*, *11*(1), 135–148.

Golumbia, D. (2017). *The politics of Bitcoin: Software as right-wing extremism* (1st ed.). Minnesota, MN: University of Minnesota Press.

Granovetter, M. (1985). Economic action and social structure: The problem of embeddedness. *American Journal of Sociology*, *91*(3), 481–510.

Granovetter, M. (1992). Economic institutions as social constructions: A framework for analysis. *Acta Sociologica*, *35*, 3–11.

Granovetter, M. (2017). *Society and economy: Framework and principles* (1st ed.). Cambridge, MA: Harvard University Press.

Greenberg, A. (2013). An interview with a digital drug lord: The Silk Road's dread pirate Roberts (Q & A). *Forbes*, August 14. Retrieved from https://www.forbes.com/sites/andygreenberg/2013/08/14/an-interview-with-a-digital-drug-lord-the-silk-roads-dread-pirate-roberts-qa/#568429a75732

Greenberg, A. (2014). Inside the "DarkMarket" prototype, a Silk Road the FBI can never seize. *Wired*, April. Retrieved from https://www.wired.com/2014/04/darkmarket/

Greenberg, A. (2018). How Dutch police took over Hansa, a top dark web market. *Wired*, August. Retrieved from https://www.wired.com/story/hansa-dutch-police-sting-operation/

Greer, A., & Ritter, A. (2019). "It's about bloody time": Perceptions of people who use drugs regarding drug law reform. *International Journal of Drug Policy*, *64*, 40–46.

Hardy, R. A., & Norgaard, J. R. (2015). Reputation in the Internet black market: An empirical and theoretical analysis of the Deep Web. *Journal of Institutional Economics*, *12*(June), 1–25. https://doi.org/10.1017/S1744137415000454

Harlev, M. A., Sun Yin, H., Langenheldt, K. C., Mukkamala, R., & Vatrapu, R. (2018). Breaking bad: De-anonymising entity types on the bitcoin blockchain using supervised machine learning. In *Proceedings of the 51st Hawaii international conference on system sciences* (p. 3497).

Harrison, J. R., Roberts, D. L., & Hernandez-Castro, J. C. (2016). Assessing the extent and nature of wildlife trade on the darkweb. *Conservation Biology*, *30*(4), 900–904. https://doi.org/10.1111/cobi.12707

Hepp, A., Breiter, A., & Friemel, T. N. (2018). Digital traces in context: An introduction. *International Journal of Communication*, *12*, 439–449.

Herley, C., & Florêncio, D. (2010). Nobody sells gold for the price of silver: Dishonesty, uncertainty and the underground economy. In *Economics of information security and privacy* (pp. 33–53). Springer. https://doi.org/10.1007/978-1-4419-6967-5_3

Holt, T. J., & Dupont, B. (2019). Exploring the Factors Associated With Rejection From a Closed Cybercrime Community. *International Journal of Offender Therapy and Comparative Criminology*, *63*(8), 1127–1147. https://doi.org/10.1177/0306624X18811101

Holt, T. J., Smirnova, O., & Chua, Y.-T. (2016). *Data thieves in action: Examining the international market for stolen personal information*. Springer.

Holt, T. J., Smirnova, O., Chua, Y. T., & Copes, H. (2015). Examining the risk reduction strategies of actors in online criminal markets. *Global Crime*, *16*(2), 81–103. https://doi.org/10.1080/17440572.2015.1013211

Horton-Eddison, M., & Di Cristofaro, M. (2017). *Policy brief 11: Hard interventions and innovation in crypto-drug markets: The escrow example*. Swansea. Retrieved from http://www.swansea.ac.uk/media/Escrow_PB11_GDPO_AUGUST2017.pdf

Hurley, R. (2017). Drug policy isn't working, medical leaders and lawmakers agree. *BMJ (Online)*, *358*, 1.

Hurley, R. (2018). Illicit drug use should not be a crime, says Royal College of Physicians. *BMJ (Online)*, *361*, 1–2.

Hutchings, A. (2014). Crime from the keyboard: Organised cybercrime, co-offending, initiation and knowledge transmission. *Crime, Law and Social Change*, *62*(1), 1–20. https://doi.org/10.1007/s10611-014-9520-z

Hutchings, A., & Holt, T. J. (2017). The online stolen data market: Disruption and intervention approaches. *Global Crime*, *18*(1), 11–30. https://doi.org/10.1080/17440572.2016.1197123

ITU. (2019). *Percentage of individuals using the Internet*. Geneva. Retrieved from https://www.itu.int/en/ITU-D/Statistics/Pages/stat/default.aspx

Jacques, S., & Wright, R. (2008). The relevance of peace studies to studies of drug market violence. *Criminology*, *46*(1), 221–254. https://doi.org/10.1111/j.1745-9125.2008.00102.x

Jacques, S., & Wright, R. (2011). Informal control and illicit drug trade. *Criminology*, *49*(3), 729–765. https://doi.org/10.1111/j.1745-9125.2011.00234.x

Kamphausen, G., & Werse, B. (2019). Digital figurations in the online trade of illicit drugs: A qualitative content analysis of darknet forums. *International Journal of Drug Policy*, https://doi.org/10.1016/j.drugpo.2019.04.011

Kowalski, M., Hooker, C., & Barratt, M. J. (2019). Should we smoke it for you as well? An ethnographic analysis of a drug cryptomarket environment. *International Journal of Drug Policy, Online First.*

Krebs, B. (2014). *Spam nation: The inside story of organized cybercrime-from global epidemic to your front door*. Naperville, IL: Sourcebooks, Inc.

Kruithof, K., Aldridge, J., Décary-Hétu, D., Sim, M., Dujso, E., & Hoorens, S. (2016). *Internet-facilitated drugs trade: An analysis of the size, scope and the role of the Netherlands*. Santa Monica, CA. Retrieved from http://www.rand.org/pubs/research_reports/RR1607.html

Krylova, Y. (2019). The rise of darknet markets in the digital age: Building trust and reputation. In M. Brown & L. Hersey (Eds.), *Returning to interpersonal dialogue and understanding human communication in the digital age* (pp. 1–24). Hershy, PA: IGI Global.

Kueppers, V., & Cooke, C. (2015). 25I-NBOMe related death in Australia: A case report. *Forensic Science International*, *249*, e15–e18.

Kuzuno, H., & Karam, C. (2017). Blockchain explorer: An analytical process and investigation environment for bitcoin. In *2017 APWG symposium on electronic crime research (eCrime)* (pp. 9–16). IEEE. https://doi.org/10.1109/ECRIME.2017.7945049

Ladegaard, I. (2017a). "I pray that we will find a way to carry on this dream": How a law enforcement crackdown united an online community. *Critical Sociology*, *45*(4–5), 631–646. https://doi.org/10.1177/0896920517735670

Ladegaard, I. (2017b). Instantly hooked? freebies and samples of opioids, cannabis, MDMA, and other drugs in an illicit e-commerce market. *Journal of Drug Issues*, *48*(2), 1–20. https://doi.org/10.1177/0022042617746975

Ladegaard, I. (2017c). We know where you are, what you are doing and we will catch you. *The British Journal of Criminology*, *4*, 175–192. https://doi.org/10.1093/bjc/azx021

Ladegaard, I. (2019). Crime displacement in digital drug markets. *International Journal of Drug Policy*, *63*, 113–121. https://doi.org/10.1016/j.drugpo.2018.09.013

Langley, P., & Leyshon, A. (2017). Platform capitalism: The intermediation and capitalization of digital economic circulation. *Finance and Society*, *3*(1), 11–31. https://doi.org/10.2218/finsoc.v3i1.1936

Lavorgna, A. (2014). Wildlife trafficking in the Internet age. *Crime Science*, *3*(1), 1–12. https://doi.org/10.1186/s40163-014-0005-2

Littlejohn, C., Baldacchino, A., Schifano, F., & Deluca, P. (2005). Internet pharmacies and online prescription drug sales: A cross-sectional study. *Drugs: Education, Prevention and Policy*, *12*(1), 75–80. https://doi.org/10.1080/0968763042000275326

Locker, T. (2015). The rise and fall of shiny flakes, Germany's online drug market. *VICE Motherboard*, March 23. Retrieved from https://motherboard.vice.com/en_us/article/the-rise-and-fall-of-shiny-flakes-germanys-online-drug-market

Lorenzo-Dus, N., & Cristofaro, M. Di. (2018). 'I know this whole market is based on the trust you put in me and I don't take that lightly': Trust, community and discourse in crypto-drug markets. https://doi.org/10.1177/1750481318771429

Ludlow, P. (2001). New foundations: On the emergence of sovereign cyberstates and their governance structures. In P. Ludlow (Ed.), *Crypto anarchy, cyberstates and pirate utopias* (Kindle edition, 1st ed.). Cambridge, MA: The MIT Press.

Lusthaus, J. (2012). Trust in the world of cybercrime. *Global Crime*, *13*(2), 71–94. https://doi.org/10.1080/17440572.2012.674183

Maddox, A., Barratt, M. J., Allen, M., & Lenton, S. (2016). Constructive activism in the dark web: cryptomarkets and illicit drugs in the digital 'demimonde.' *Information, Communication & Society*, *19*(1), 111–126. https://doi.org/10.1080/1369118X.2015.1093531

Malik, N. (2019). How the Darknet can be used by terrorists to obtain weapons. *Forbes*. Retrived from https://www.forbes.com/sites/nikitamalik/2019/01/15/how-the-darknet-can-be-used-by-terrorists-to-obtain-weapons/#3004bb5662cd

Markoff, J. (2005). *What the Dormouse said: How the sixties counterculture shaped the personal computerIndustry*. Penguin.

Martin, J. (2014a). *Drugs on the dark net: How cryptomarkets are transforming the global trade in illicit drugs* (Kindle edition). Palgrave Macmillan.

Martin, J. (2014b). Lost on the Silk Road: Online drug distribution and the "cryptomarket." *Criminology and Criminal Justice*, *14*(3), 351–367. https://doi.org/10.1177/1748895813505234

Martin, J. (2018). Cryptomarkets, systemic violence and the 'gentrification hypothesis.' *Addiction*, *113*(5), 797–798. https://doi.org/10.1111/add.14029

Martin, J., & Christin, N. (2016). Ethics in cryptomarket research. *International Journal of Drug Policy*, *35*, 84–91. https://doi.org/10.1016/j.drugpo.2016.05.006

Martin, J., Cunliffe, J. D., Décary-Hétu, D., & Aldridge, J. (2018a). Effect of restricting the legal supply of prescription opioids on buying through online illicit marketplaces: Interrupted time series analysis. *BMJ (Online)*, *361*. https://doi.org/10.1136/bmj.k2270

Martin, J., Cunliffe, J. D., Décary-Hétu, D., & Aldridge, J. (2018b). *The International Darknet drugs trade – A regional analysis of cryptomarkets*. Canberra, Australia: Australian Institute of Criminology. Retrieved from https://aic.gov.au/publications/rr/rr10

Martinez, M., Kmetonyová, D., & Běláčková, V. (2016). A method for exploring the number of online ships selling new psychoactive substances: Initital I-TREND project results. In *The internet and drug markets* (pp. 97–106). Luxembourg: European Monitoring Centre for Drugs and Drug Addiction.

Masson, K., & Bancroft, A. (2018). 'Nice people doing shady things': Drugs and the morality of exchange in the darknet cryptomarkets. *International Journal of Drug Policy*, *58*(May), 78–84. https://doi.org/https://doi.org/10.1016/j.drugpo.2018.05.008

May, C. (2017). *Transnational crime and the developing world*. Global financial integrity. Retreived from https://gfintegrity.org/report/transnational-crime-and-the-developing-world/

May, T. (1994). The cyphernomicon: Cypherpunks FAQ and more. Retrieved from https://cpunks.wordpress.com/cypherpunks-faq/

May, T. (2001a). Crypto anarchy and virtual communities. In P. Ludlow (Ed.), *Crypto anarchy, cyberstates and pirate utopias* (Kindle edition, 1st ed.). Cambridge, MA: The MIT Press.

May, T. (2001b). The crypto anarchist manifesto. In P. Ludlow (Ed.), *Crypto anarchy, cyberstates and pirate utopias* (Kindle edition). Cambridge, MA: MIT Press.

Moeller, K., Munksgaard, R., & Demant, J. (2017). Flow my FE the vendor said: Exploring violent and fraudulent resource exchanges on cryptomarkets for illicit drugs. *American Behavioral Scientist*, *61*(11), 1427–1450. https://doi.org/10.1177/0002764217734269

Moore, D., & Rid, T. (2016). Cryptopolitik and the Darknet. *Survival*, *58*(1), 7–38.

Mörch, C.-M., Côté, L.-P., Corthésy-Blondin, L., Plourde-Léveillé, L., Dargis, L., & Mishara, B. L. (2018). The Darknet and suicide. *Journal of Affective Disorders*, *241*, 127–132. https://doi.org/10.1016/j.jad.2018.08.028

Morselli, C., Décary-Hétu, D., Paquet-Clouston, M., & Aldridge, J. (2017). Conflict management in illicit drug cryptomarkets. *International Criminal Justice Review*, *27*(4), 237–254. https://doi.org/10.1177/1057567717709498

Mounteney, J., Cunningham, A., Groshkova, T., Sedefov, R., & Griffiths, P. (2017). Looking to the future – More concern than optimism that cryptomarkets will reduce drug-related harms. *Addiction*, *113*(5), 799–800. https://doi.org/10.1111/add.14056

Moyle, L., Childs, A., Coomber, R., & Barratt, M. J. (2019). #Drugsforsale: An exploration of the use of social media and encrypted messaging apps to supply and access drugs. *International Journal of Drug Policy*, *63*, 101–110. https://doi.org/10.1016/j.drugpo.2018.08.005

Munksgaard, R., Bakken, S., & Demant, J. (2017). Risk perception in emerging markets for illicit substances in Scandinavia – The effect of available information through online communities. In *NSFK Seminar*. Retrieved from https://www.researchgate.net/profile/Jakob_Demant/publication/317688386_Risk_perception_in_emerging_markets_for_illicit_substances_in_Scandinavia_-_The_effect_of_available_information_through_online_communities/links/59490c63a6fdcc70635e52f5/Risk-percepti

Munksgaard, R., & Demant, J. (2016). Mixing politics and crime – The prevalence and decline of political discourse on the cryptomarket. *International Journal of Drug Policy*, *35*, 77–83. https://doi.org/10.1016/j.drugpo.2016.04.021

Munksgaard, R., Demant, J., & Branwen, G. (2016). A replication and methodological critique of the study "Evaluating drug trafficking on the Tor Network." *International Journal of Drug Policy*, *35*, 92–96. https://doi.org/10.1016/j.drugpo.2016.02.027

Nakamoto, S. (2008). Bitcoin: A peer-to-peer electronic cash system. Retrieved from https://bitcoin.org/bitcoin.pdf

New Zealand Police. (2016). Kiwi darknet illegal drug buyers identified during worldwide operation. Retrieved from http://www.police.govt.nz/news/release/kiwi-darknet-illegal-drug-buyers-identified-during-worldwide-operation?nondesktop. Accessed on June 12, 2017.

Norbutas, L. (2018). Offline constraints in online drug marketplaces: An exploratory analysis of a cryptomarket trade network. *International Journal of Drug Policy*, *56*, 92–100. https://doi.org/10.1016/j.drugpo.2018.03.016

Nurmi, J., Kaskela, T., Perälä, J., & Oksanen, A. (2017). Seller's reputation and capacity on the illicit drug markets: 11-month study on the Finnish version of the Silk Road. *Drug and Alcohol Dependence*, *178*, 201–207. https://doi.org/10.1016/j.drugalcdep.2017.05.018

Nutt, D., Saulsbury, W., & Blakemore, C. (2007). Development of a rational scale to assess the harm of drugs of potential misuse. *The Lancet*, *369*(9566), 1047–1053.

Ormsby, E. (2014). *Silk Road* (Kindle edition). Victoria, Australia: Palgrave Macmillan.

Ormsby, E. (2015). Waiting in the Red Room. Retrieved from https://allthingsvice.com/2015/08/29/waiting-in-the-red-room/. Accessed on April 25, 2019.

Ormsby, E. (2016). The curious case of Besa Mafia. Retrieved from https://allthingsvice.com/2016/05/14/the-curious-case-of-besa-mafia/

Ormsby, E. (2018). *Darkest web*. Crows Nest, NSW: Allen & Unwin. Retrieved from https://www.allenandunwin.com/browse/books/general-books/true-crime/Darkest-Web-Eileen-Ormsby-9781760297855

Orsolini, L., Francesconi, G., Papanti, D., Giorgetti, A., & Schifano, F. (2015). Profiling online recreational/prescription drugs' customers and overview of drug vending virtual marketplaces. *Human Psychopharmacology: Clinical and Experimental*, *30*(4), 302–318. https://doi.org/10.1002/hup.2466

Pace, J. (2017). Exchange relations on the dark web. *Critical Studies in Media Communication*, *34*(1), 1–13. https://doi.org/10.1080/15295036.2016.1243249

Paoli, G. (2018). *The trade in small arms and light weapons on the Dark Web*. UNODA Occasional Paper No. 32.

Paquet-Clouston, M., Décary-Hétu, D., & Morselli, C. (2018). Assessing market competition and vendors' size and scope on AlphaBay. *International Journal of Drug Policy*, *54*, 87–98. https://doi.org/10.1016/j.drugpo.2018.01.003

Parker, H. J., Aldridge, J., & Measham, F. (1998). *Illegal leisure: The normalization of adolescent recreational drug use*. Routledge.

Peacock, A., Leung, J., Larney, S., Colledge, S., Hickman, M., Rehm, J., ... Degenhardt, L. (2018). Global statistics on alcohol, tobacco and illicit drug use: 2017 status report. *Addiction*, *113*(10), 1905–1926.

Popper, N. (2017a). Opioid dealers embrace the dark web to send deadly drugs by mail. *The New York Times*, June 10. Retrieved from https://www.nytimes.com/2017/06/10/business/dealbook/opioid-dark-web-drug-overdose.html?_r=0&module=inline

Popper, N. (2017b). Hansa market, a dark web marketplace, bans the sale of fentanyl. *The New York Times*, July 18.

Porter, K. (2018). Analyzing the DarkNetMarkets subreddit for evolutions of tools and trends using LDA topic modeling. *Digital Investigation*, *26*, S87–S97. https://doi.org/10.1016/J.DIIN.2018.04.023

Potter, G. (2009). Exploring retail-level drug distribution: Social supply, "real" dealers and the user/dealer interface. In Z. Demetrovics, J. Fountain, & L. Kraus (Eds.), *Old and new policies, theories, research methods and drug users across Europe* (pp. 50–74). Lengerich, Germany: Pabst Science Publishers.

Power, M. (2019). Police thought they beat the darknet drug markets – They Didn't. *VICE*.

Przepiorka, W. (2013). Buyers pay for and sellers invest in a good reputation: More evidence from eBay. *The Journal of Socio-Economics*, *42*, 31–42. https://doi.org/10.1016/J.SOCEC.2012.11.004

Przepiorka, W., Norbutas, L., & Corten, R. (2017). Order without Law: Reputation promotes cooperation in a cryptomarket for illegal drugs. *European Sociological Review*, *33*(6), 752–764. https://doi.org/10.1093/esr/jcx072

Quintana, P., Ventura, M., Grifell, M., Palma, A., Galindo, L., Fornís, I., … Torrens, M. (2016). The hidden web and the fentanyl problem: Detection of ocfentanil as an adulterant in heroin. *International Journal of Drug Policy*, *40*, 78–83. https://doi.org/10.1016/j.drugpo.2016.10.006

RCMP. (2016). The RCMP and law enforcement agencies around the world collaborate on international Darknet marketplace enforcement. Retrieved from http://www.rcmp-grc.gc.ca/en/news/2016/1/the-rcmp-and-law-enforcement-agencies-the-world-collaborate-international-darknet. Accessed on June 12, 2017.

reddit. (2018, March 21). New addition to site-wide rules regarding the use of Reddit to conduct transactions. *R/Announcements*. Retrieved from https://www.reddit.com/r/announcements/comments/863xcj/new_addition_to_sitewide_rules_regarding_the_use/

Reddit Policy. (2018). New addition to site-wide rules regarding the use of Reddit to conduct transactions: Announcements. Retrieved from https://www.reddit.com/r/announcements/comments/863xcj/new_addition_to_sitewide_rules_regarding_the_use/. Accessed on March 20, 2019.

Resnick, P., Kuwabara, K., Zeckhauser, R., & Friedman, E. (2000). Reputation systems. *Communications of the ACM*, *43*(12), 45–48.

Reuter, P., & Greenfield, V. (2001). Measuring global drug markets: How good are the numbers and why should we care about them? *World Economics*, 2(4), 159–173.

Reuter, P., & Kleiman, M. A. (1986). Risks and prices: An economic analysis of drug enforcement. *Crime and Justice*, 7, 289–340. https://doi.org/10.1086/449116

Rhumorbarbe, D., Staehli, L., Broséus, J., Rossy, Q., Esseiva, P., Damien, R., ... Pierre, E. (2016). Buying drugs on a Darknet market: A better deal? Studying the online illicit drug market through the analysis of digital, physical and chemical data. *Forensic Science International*, *267*(August), 173–182. https://doi.org/10.1016/j.forsciint.2016.08.032

Rhumorbarbe, D., Werner, D., Gilliéron, Q., Staehli, L., Broséus, J., & Rossy, Q. (2018). Characterising the online weapons trafficking on cryptomarkets. *Forensic Science International*, *283*, 16–20. https://doi.org/10.1016/j.forsciint.2017.12.008

Rizzo, P. (2014a). Black market cannabis road hacked, $100k in bitcoin lost. *CoinDesk*.

Rizzo, P. (2014b). Silk road 2.0 claims 80% of stolen bitcoin repaid to customers. *CoinDesk*.

Roberts, D. P. (2012). Armory discussion forum.

Rudd, R. (2016). Increases in drug and opioid-involved overdose deaths – United States, 2010–2015. *MMWR. Morbidity and Mortality Weekly Report*, *65*(50–51), 1445–1452.

Sanchez-Rola, I., Balzarotti, D., & Santos, I. (2017). The onions have eyes. In *Proceedings of the 26th international conference on world wide web – WWW '17* (pp. 1251–1260). New York, NY: ACM Press. https://doi.org/10.1145/3038912.3052657

Schonlau, M., & Couper, M. P. (2017). Options for conducting web surveys. *Statistical Science*, *32*(2), 279–292. https://doi.org/10.1214/16-STS597

Scott, N., Caulkins, J., Ritter, A., Quinn, C., & Dietze, P. (2015). High-frequency drug purity and price series as tools for explaining drug trends and harms in Victoria, Australia. *Addiction*, *110*(1), 120–128.

Sindicich, N., Stafford, J., & Breen, C. (2016). *Australian trends in ecstasy and related drug markets 2015. Findings from the ecstasy and related drugs reporting system (EDRS)*. Australian Drug Trends Series. Sydney, Australia.

Søgaard, T., Kolind, T., Haller, M., & Hunt, G. (2019). Ring and bring drug services: Delivery dealing and the social life of a drug phone. *International Journal of Drug Policy*, *69*(8–15), 8–15.

Soska, K., & Christin, N. (2015). Measuring the longitudinal evolution of the online anonymous marketplace ecosystem. In *24th USENIX security symposium (USENIX security 15)* (pp. 33–48). https://doi.org/10.1007/s00253-017-8456-5

Sotirakopoulos, N. (2017). Cryptomarkets as a libertarian counter-conduct of resistance. *European Journal of Social Theory*, *21*, 189–206. https://doi.org/10.1177/1368431017718534

Soudijn, M. R. J., & Zegers, B. C. H. T. (2012). Cybercrime and virtual offender convergence settings. *Trends in Organized Crime*, *15*(2–3), 111–129. https://doi.org/10.1007/s12117-012-9159-z

Spitters, M., Verbruggen, S., & Staalduinen, M. Van. (2014). Towards a comprehensive insight into the thematic organization of the tor hidden services. In *Proceedings – 2014 IEEE joint intelligence and security informatics conference, JISIC 2014* (pp. 220–223). https://doi.org/10.1109/JISIC.2014.40

Stevens, H. (2016). Social media as a platform for crime. *NSfK's 58. Research Seminar*. Retrieved from http://www.nsfk.org/Portals/0/Archive/Report NSfK Research Seminar 2016 FINAL.pdf#page=440

Sykes, G. M., & Matza, D. (1957). Techniques of neutralization: A theory of delinquency. *American Sociological Review*, *22*(6), 664. https://doi.org/10.2307/2089195

Tadelis, S. (2016). Reputation and feedback systems in online platform markets. *Annual Review of Economics*, *8*(1), 321–340. https://doi.org/10.1146/annurev-economics-080315-015325

Tor Project. (2019). Tor: Overview. Retrieved from https://www.torproject.org/about/overview. Accessed on December 10, 2015.

Tzanetakis, M. (2018a). Comparing cryptomarkets for drugs. A characterisation of sellers and buyers over time. *International Journal of Drug Policy*, *56*(0), 176–186. https://doi.org/10.1016/j.drugpo.2018.01.022

Tzanetakis, M. (2018b). Social order of anonymous digital markets: Towards an economic sociology of cryptomarkets. In G. Potter, K. Fountain, & D. Korf (Eds.), *Place, space and time in European drug use, markets and policy* (pp. 61–80). Lengerich: Pabst Science Publishers.

Tzanetakis, M., Kamphausen, G., Werse, B., & von Laufenberg, R. (2016). The transparency paradox. Building trust, resolving disputes and optimising logistics on conventional and online drugs markets. *International Journal of Drug Policy*, *35*, 58–68. https://doi.org/10.1016/j.drugpo.2015.12.010

Union, I. T. (2013). *Percentage of individuals using the Internet 2000–2012*. Geneva.

UNODC. (2017). *World Drug Report 2017*.

UNODC. (2018). *World Drug Report 2018*.

Van Buskirk, J., Bruno, R., Dobbins, T., Breen, C., Burns, L., Naicker, S., & Roxburgh, A. (2017). The recovery of online drug markets following law enforcement and other disruptions. *Drug and Alcohol Dependence*, *173*, 159–162. https://doi.org/10.1016/j.drugalcdep.2017.01.004

Van Buskirk, J., Naicker, S., Roxburgh, A., Bruno, R., & Burns, L. (2016). Who sells what? Country specific differences in substance availability on the agora cryptomarket. *International Journal of Drug Policy*, *35*, 16–23. https://doi.org/10.1016/j.drugpo.2016.07.004

Van Buskirk, J., Roxburgh, A., Bruno, R., Naicker, S., Lenton, S., Sutherland, R., … Burns, L. (2016). Characterising dark net marketplace purchasers in a sample of regular psychostimulant users. *International Journal of Drug Policy*, *35*, 32–37.

Van Buskirk, J., Roxburgh, A., Farrell, M., & Burns, L. (2014). The closure of the Silk Road: what has this meant for online drug trading? *Addiction*, *109*(4), 517–518. https://doi.org/10.1111/add.12422

van der Gouwe, D., Brunt, T. M., van Laar, M., & van der Pol, P. (2017). Purity, adulteration and price of drugs bought on-line versus off-line in the Netherlands. *Addiction*, *112*(4), 640–648. https://doi.org/10.1111/add.13720

van der Gouwe, D., Rigter, S., & Brunt, T. M. (2018). Focus on cryptomarkets and online reviews too narrow to debate harms of drugs bought online. *Addiction*, *113*(5), 798–799. https://doi.org/10.1111/add.14060

Van Hout, M. C., & Bingham, T. (2013a). "Silk Road", the virtual drug marketplace: A single case study of user experiences. *International Journal of Drug Policy*, *24*(5), 385–391. https://doi.org/10.1016/j.drugpo.2013.01.005

Van Hout, M. C., & Bingham, T. (2013b). "Surfing the Silk Road": A study of users' experiences. *International Journal of Drug Policy*, *24*(6), 524–529.

Van Hout, M. C., & Bingham, T. (2014). Responsible vendors, intelligent consumers: Silk Road, the online revolution in drug trading. *International Journal of Drug Policy*, *25*(2), 183–189.

Van Hout, M. C., & Hearne, E. (2017). New psychoactive substances (NPS) on cryptomarket fora: An exploratory study of characteristics of forum activity between NPS buyers and vendors. *International Journal of Drug Policy*, *40*, 102–110. https://doi.org/10.1016/j.drugpo.2016.11.007

van Wegberg, R., & Verburgh, T. (2018). Lost in the dream? Measuring the effects of operation Bayonet on vendors migrating to Dream Market. In *Evolution of the Darknet Workshop at the Web Science Conference (WebSci 18)* (pp. 1–5).

Venturini, T., & Latour, B. (2009). The social fabric the social fabric: Digital traces and quali-quantitative methods. In *Futur En Seine 2009, Cap Digita*, May 2009, Paris, France (p. 1293394). https://doi.org/<hal-01293394>

Walsh, C. (2011). Drugs, the Internet and change. *Journal of Psychoactive Drugs*, *43*(1), 55–63. https://doi.org/10.1080/02791072.2011.566501

Warner, M., Trinidad, J. P., Bastian, B. A., Miniño, A. M., & Hedegaard, H. (2016). *Drugs most frequently involved in drug overdose deaths: United States, 2010–2014*. Hyattsville, MD.

Weimann, G. (2015). Going dark: Terrorism on the Dark Web. *Studies in Conflict & Terrorism*, *0*(3), 1–24. https://doi.org/10.1080/1057610X.2015.1119546

Winder, D. (2019). Did a bitcoin exit scam cause dark web wall street market crash? *Forbes*, May 3. Retrieved from https://www.forbes.com/sites/daveywinder/2019/05/03/did-a-bitcoin-exit-scam-cause-dark-web-wall-street-market-crash/#6ed7b6096b73

Winstock, A. R., Barratt, M. J., Maier, L., Aldridge, J., Zhuparris, A., Davies, E., … Ferris, J. A. (2019). *Global Drug Survey 2019 Key Findings Report*.

Wright, J. (2019). Darknet usage in the illegal wildlife trade. *Tools and Guidance, Oxford Martin Programme on the Illegal Wildlife Trade*. https://doi.org/10.31235/OSF.IO/FGR9D

Zajácz, R. (2017). Silk Road: The market beyond the reach of the state. *The Information Society*, *33*(1), 23–34. https://doi.org/10.1080/01972243.2016.1248612

Zaunseder, A., & Bancroft, A. (2019). The fuzzy ideological and social space of the cryptomarkets: Libertarian ideology, agorism and exchange performances. In *Drogen, Darknet und Organisierte Kriminalität* (pp. 137–160). Nomos Verlagsgesellschaft mbH & Co. KG. https://doi.org/10.5771/9783845282831-137

Zetter, K. (2012). 8 suspects arrested in online drug market sting. *Wired*, April. Retrieved from https://www.wired.com/2012/04/online-drug-market-takedown/

Zimmermann, P. (1999). Why i wrote PGP. Retrieved from https://www.philzimmermann.com/EN/essays/WhyIWrotePGP.html

INDEX

Note: Page numbers followed by "*n*" with numbers indicate notes.

www.ingramcontent.com/pod-product-compliance
Lightning Source LLC
Chambersburg PA
CBHW071323180926
51611CB00002B/32
* 9 7 8 1 8 3 8 6 7 0 3 3 7 *